Check and test

Religious Studies

Christianity, philosophy and ethics, and moral issues

Jon Mayled and Libby Ahluwalia

Published by BBC Educational Publishing,
BBC White City, 80 Wood Lane, London W12 0TT.

First published 2002

Colour reproduction by Spectrum Colour, England

Printed and bound by Poligrafico Dehonanio, Italy.

Contents

War, peace and justice

Evil and suffering

Science and religion

Religion and the media

The Church

Sacraments

Christian life

The Christian year

Answers

About GCSE Bitesize

- GCSE Bitesize is a revision service designed to help you achieve success in your exams with **books, television programmes** and a website at **www.bbc.co.uk/education/revision**.
- It's called Bitesize because it breaks revision into bite-sized chunks to make it easier to learn.

How to use this book

- This book explains and tests the **100 things you must know** for GCSE Religious Studies (Christianity, philosophy and ethics, and moral issues). It provides:
  - the key information you need in the 'Check the facts' sections
  - questions to test your understanding in the 'Test yourself' sections.
- Use this book to check you know this area of GCSE Religious Studies. If you can prove to yourself that you're confident with these key ideas, you'll know that you're on track with your learning.
- You can use this book to test yourself:
  - during your GCSE course
  - at the end of the course during revision.
- As you revise you can use Check and Test in several ways:
  - as a summary of the essential information on each of the 100 topics to help you revise those areas
  - to check your progress: test to see which topics you're confident with
  - as a way to keep track and plan your time: you can aim to check and test a set number of topics each time you revise, knowing how many you need to cover in total and how much time you've got.

GCSE Bitesize revision materials

There's nothing like variety for making revision more interesting, and covering a topic from several different angles is an ideal way to make it stick in your head. There are lots of GCSE Bitesize Revision materials in different media, so take take your choice and make learning enjoyable.

GCSE Bitesize Revision: Religious Studies is a **book** which contains the key information and skills you need to revise, plus lots of tips and practice questions to help you improve your results. GCSE Bitesize Revision: Religious Studies ISBN: 0 563 54473 2

The GCSE Bitesize Revision: Religious Studies **website** provides even more explanation and practice to help you revise.

Website address: www.bbc.co.uk/education/revision

The Religious Studies exam

In the Religious Studies exam, most questions are very straightforward and there are really three main types:

1 There are simple questions, where you may be asked to define a key term, a teaching, or a particular aspect of a religion or belief.

2 There are some questions where you have to apply your knowledge to a particular situation. These questions may ask you to explain what is meant by a particular topic within a religion or ask you what the effect of a particular belief might be on the life of a member of that religion.

3 There are also questions which ask for your opinion about a religious topic. You will usually be asked to consider different points of view and to offer evidence or arguments to support these.

Always read the questions carefully to see exactly what is required. If you are pressed for time, give shorter answers to all the questions rather than long answers to only the easy ones. In that way, you will gain more marks!

Good luck!

Check the facts

The life of Jesus is an essential part of the Christian faith and there are a number of key events that are very important.

Christians believe that Jesus Christ was the Son of God.

Jesus was born sometime between 8 and 6 BCE in the town of Bethlehem in Judaea, Palestine. His mother was a young woman called Mary. Jesus' father was a carpenter called Joseph, but the Bible teaches that his real father was God himself and that Mary was told of this by a visit from the Archangel Gabriel. It was God who made Mary pregnant so Jesus was born of a virgin.

Just before Jesus was born, a census was being carried out by the Roman authorities. For Joseph, this meant that he had to travel from his home in Nazareth to the city of Bethlehem, and it was here that Jesus was born in a stable.

Jesus was taken to the Temple in Jerusalem to be circumcised like all young Jewish boys and, later, at the age of twelve, he travelled with his parents to Jerusalem, where **he spoke to the elders of the Temple and told them that he was in his Father's house.**

We know nothing else of Jesus until he was aged about thirty. It was then that his work began. He visited his cousin, John the Baptist, who was living the life of a hermit in the desert and baptizing people in the River Jordan. **Jesus was baptized by John and, from this time on, his followers began to believe him to be the Son of God.**

Immediately after the Baptism, **Jesus went into the wilderness for forty days to prepare himself for his ministry**, and here he was tempted by the devil. **He gathered around him a group of men who are known as the Twelve Disciples**:

- Simon Peter
- Andrew
- John
- Philip
- James the son of Zebedee
- Bartholomew
- Thomas
- Matthew
- James the son of Alphaeus,
- Thaddaeus
- Simon
- Judas Iscariot.

They were all working men from Galilee, some were fishermen and one, Matthew, was a tax-collector.

Jesus preached mostly in the open. **He performed many other miracles** during his ministry in Galilee, in particular healing sick people, making the lame walk and the blind see. Most of his teaching was in **parables**. These were stories which his listeners could easily understand, but which had a very important message.

Jesus angered the Jewish authorities, particularly by his teaching that, despite the fourth commandment of Moses – 'Remember the Sabbath and keep it holy', – it was still doing God's will to heal the sick on the Sabbath. Apart from this, however, the Jewish priests were alarmed by **the claim that Jesus was the Messiah.** They expected the Messiah to be a king leading an army to free them from the rule of the Romans.

At the time of the feast of the Passover, Jesus made his entry into Jerusalem riding on a donkey while the crowds sang and laid palm branches in his path. He threw the money-lenders and traders out of the Temple and preached in Jerusalem for a few final days. Then, after celebrating a special meal with his disciples (the **Last Supper**), he was betrayed to the soldiers of the High Priest by **Judas Iscariot**. He was tried by the High Priest and the elders (the **Sanhedrin**) and was then taken before **Pontius Pilate, the Roman Governor**.

Pilate tried to save Jesus from the Jews but they were so insistent on his guilt that he was finally forced to sentence him to death. Jesus was taken to a hill called **Calvary** outside of Jerusalem and there, on **Good Friday**, he was nailed to a cross and **crucified**.

A rich follower of Jesus, **Joseph of Arimathaea**, begged Pilate for Jesus' body and had it taken away and placed in a private tomb. The Sabbath began that evening, so it was not until Sunday morning that anyone could visit the tomb.

When three women, also followers of Jesus, arrived at the tomb they found that the stone covering the entrance had been rolled away. At first they thought that someone had stolen the body but, shortly afterwards, they and the disciples met Jesus, **who had risen from the dead, as had been prophesied in the Old Testament**.

Jesus stayed with his disciples for another forty days and then **they saw him rise up into heaven to rejoin his Father**.

Test yourself

1 Choose two events from the life of Jesus and explain why they are still important to Christians today.

2 Why do you think that the Jews in Jerusalem wanted Jesus to be executed?

Check the facts

Christians believe that Jesus was the Son of God. They believe that Jesus was **God incarnate**, which means God in human form. They also believe that God came to the Earth as a man to live amongst other people, to teach them and to share in their sufferings.

The Jewish scriptures (**Old Testament**) predicted that one day a **Messiah** would come, who would bring peace to the world and be a leader for the Jews. Christians believe that when the Messiah was prophesied, the prophets were talking about Jesus. **'Christ' and 'Messiah' both mean 'anointed one'** – a person was anointed with oil if they were blessed.

Christians believe that Jesus sacrificed himself by dying on the cross, on behalf of all of humanity. **They believe that because Jesus died, people could be forgiven for their sins and would be able to have a complete relationship with God.** They believe that although the first man, Adam, disobeyed God, Jesus was obedient and put right the wrong that Adam had done.

According to Christianity, Jesus was **resurrected** on **Easter Sunday**, which means he rose from the dead. **They believe that Jesus came alive again after he had been crucified and this proved that he really was the Son of God.** They believe that Jesus continues to live today and that he answers prayers. **They believe that because Jesus rose from the dead, they too can hope for eternal life with God.**

Christians believe that Jesus is the second person of the Trinity – God the Son.

Christians believe that the life of Jesus, as told in the Gospels, provides them with an example to follow.

Test yourself

1 What do Christians mean when they call Jesus 'Christ' or 'Messiah'?

2 Explain what Christians believe about Jesus as 'God incarnate'.

3 What do Christians believe happened to the relationship between God and humanity when Jesus died on the cross?

4 Why is belief in the resurrection of Jesus important for Christians?

Check the facts

Christians believe that there is only one God. They are monotheists.

Christians also believe that God can be understood in three different ways, as the three 'persons' of the Trinity: **God the Father**, **God the Son**, and **God the Holy Spirit**. This does not mean that there are three gods, but it describes three different ways in which Christians believe they can understand and experience God.

God the Father is believed to be the creator of the universe. God is also called Father as a way of showing human dependence on God to provide for them. It also shows a close and loving relationship.

God the Son refers to Jesus. Christians believe that Jesus was not just an ordinary man, but was God in human form. Christians believe that the death and resurrection of Jesus made it possible for them to have salvation.

God the Holy Spirit refers to the way in which God lives in the hearts and lives of believers. Christians believe that God sent his Holy Spirit to comfort and guide people, so that when they pray, God answers them and gives them the courage to do the right thing.

Test yourself

1 Explain in your own words what Christians mean when they talk about
a) God the Father
b) God the Son
c) God the Holy Spirit.

2 How might a Christian answer, if someone suggested that Christians believe in three different Gods?

Check the facts

Agape is a Greek word for 'love'.

Agape is love that has no conditions, but is for everyone, even if they are enemies or strangers. It involves wanting the best for the other person, and treating other people as equals because they are part of God's creation. It is believed to be the way that God loves people.

When Jesus was asked which was the most important of all the commandments, he chose two.

> 'The most important one', answered Jesus, 'is this: "Hear, O Israel, the Lord our God, the Lord is one. Love the Lord your God with all your heart and with all your soul and with all your mind and with all your strength." The second is this: "Love your neighbour as yourself." There is no commandment greater than these.' (Mark 12:29–31).

These are known as the **Two Greatest Commandments**.

Another of Jesus' teachings has become known as the **Golden Rule**:

> 'So in everything, do to others what you would have them do to you.' (Matthew 7:12)

Christians try to use this rule whenever they have moral decisions to make.

The New Testament letters also emphasise the importance of agape.

> 'And now these three remain: faith, hope and love. But the greatest of these is love.' (1 Corinthians 13:13)

Some Christians have argued that as long as people try to do the most loving thing when they are making moral choices, they will not go wrong.

Test yourself

1 What are the Two Greatest Commandments'?

2 What is the Golden Rule?

3 Explain the difference between agape and other kinds of love.

Check the facts

The two concepts of sanctity of life, and the soul, are central to Christian teaching and morality.

Sanctity of life

Christians believe that all life was created by God. The story of the **Creation** of the world is in Genesis 1–3. Here, after he has created the world, the plants and the animals, God finally creates human beings, Adam and Eve.

> Then God said, 'Let us make man in our image, in our likeness, and let them rule over the fish of the sea and the birds of the air, over the livestock, over all the Earth, and over all the creatures that move along the ground.' (Genesis 1:26–28)

This means that humans are a very important part of creation and God gives them authority over the Earth. **Because God created all life, including human beings, Christians believe that all life belongs to God and therefore is sacred.** Christianity says that '**God gives and God takes away**'.

Beliefs about the soul

Christians believe that all human beings have a 'soul'. This is the special part of someone that is given to them by God.

The soul is separate from the body and is the immortal part of a person, the part that does not die but which eventually returns to God. When God breathed life into human beings, he was giving Adam his soul.

When people do something wrong, they sometimes say: '**the soul is willing but the flesh is weak**'. They are arguing that the soul is the good part of them that knows right from wrong but that it is their body which gives in to temptation. Christianity teaches that only human beings have souls because they are made in the image of God, with the power and wisdom to know right from wrong.

Test yourself

1 Explain what Christians mean by 'sanctity of life'.

2 What is meant by the phrase 'God gives and God takes away'?

3 Explain what Christians mean by the difference between body and soul.

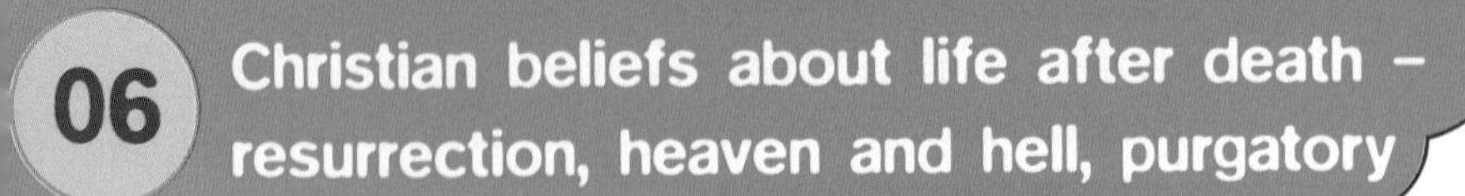

06 Christian beliefs about life after death – resurrection, heaven and hell, purgatory

Check the facts

Christians believe that when they die they will have the chance of eternal life.

This belief is found in the **Nicene Creed**, where it states that:

> We look for the resurrection of the dead, and the life of the world to come.

For most Christians, the fact that they believe in Jesus as the Son of God and follow his teachings means that they will go to heaven when they die. It is not clear whether people will go straight to heaven after death, or whether they will wait until the **Day of Judgement**. Heaven is viewed as a paradise where people will live with God.

Hell

People who have not lived a good life on Earth will be sent to hell. Christian teaching and opinions about hell have changed over time. At one time it was believed that hell was a place of fire and brimstone where people would be eternally punished by the devil. Today, many people think that hell is simply a place where people are forever deprived from seeing God and being happy. In the same way, they see heaven as being eternally in the sight of God.

Purgatory

Roman Catholics believe that there is a place between heaven and hell called purgatory. Most people are not good enough to go straight to heaven because of sins they have committed on Earth and so, instead, they are taken to purgatory where they are punished for a period of time before they are able to enter heaven.

The Bible is not clear about whether this new life after death is a physical or spiritual one.

Some people believe that they will be in heaven in their physical bodies as they were on Earth.

Other people believe that when they die it is just their souls that live on for eternity.

The **Apostles' Creed** says:

I believe... the resurrection of the body,
and the life everlasting.

The important thing to remember is the central Christian belief that the sacrifice of Jesus on the cross means that all people who follow him will have the opportunity of eternal life with God when they die.

Test yourself

1 What is purgatory?

2 What do Christians believe will happen to them when they die?

3 Explain different views of heaven and hell.

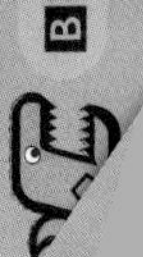

Beliefs about the nature of God

Check the facts

Christians believe that there is only one God. They are monotheists.

- Christians believe that God cannot usually be experienced with the five senses. **God is invisible.**
- They believe that **God is beyond space and time**. God can be everywhere, in the past, the present and the future. God can know everything which has happened, and everything which will happen.

Christians believe that God is omniscient, which means 'all-knowing'.

- **God is believed to be the creator of the universe and everything in it.** God keeps the world in existence, and can do anything.

Christians believe that God is omnipotent, which means 'all-powerful'.

- **God is believed to be perfectly loving and perfectly good.**
- **God is believed to be involved with the world and with everything in it, caring for individuals and keeping the universe in existence.**

God is also transcendent, which means that he is above the universe and beyond it.

Test yourself

1 Explain what is meant by the following words:
a) transcendent
b) omnipotent
c) omniscient.

2 What is the name of the doctrine which explains how God can be understood in three different ways?

3 What is the name for belief in only one God?

Check the facts

Christianity teaches that sin is to act against the will of God. If people sin they are breaking one of God's rules for how people should lead their lives.

These rules are based on the **Ten Commandments (Exodus 20:1–17)** and the **Two Greatest Commandments**:

> 'The most important one,' answered Jesus, 'is this: "Hear, O Israel, the Lord our God, the Lord is one. Love the Lord your God with all your heart and with all your soul and with all your mind and with all your strength." The second is this: "Love your neighbour as yourself." There is no commandment greater than these.'
> (Mark 12:29–31)

When a person sins they are rejecting God's love by breaking the rules he has set down for humanity. When people have not sinned they are said to be in a **state of grace**. This means that they are living according to God's will and so accepting his love.

When Jesus died willingly on the cross he **atoned** for people's sins. This means that everyone who believes that Jesus is the Son of God and who follows his teachings is freed from the punishment of their sins. **They are forgiven by God and so receive salvation.**

Test yourself

1 What is a sin?

2 What rules has God given human beings to live by?

3 Explain how Jesus' death led to salvation for human beings.

Christian attitudes towards other world religions

Check the facts

Some Christians believe that Christianity is the only true religion. They believe that people will only go to heaven if they believe that Jesus Christ is the Son of God. In John's Gospel, Jesus said:

> 'I am the way and the truth and the life. No one comes to the Father except through me.'
> (John 14:6)

Some Christians interpret this to mean that there is no other way to God except through Christianity.

Christians who hold these views often try to **convert** members of other religions to the Christian faith. They might choose to go and work as **missionaries** in other countries to persuade people to convert to Christianity instead of following a wrong religion. These Christians often say that there would be no point in Jesus dying on the cross if there were already lots of other ways to get to God. The crucifixion and resurrection are more important than this.

Learning from each other

Other Christians believe that the different world religions are not totally wrong. They might point out that Jesus was Jewish and that the Christian Old Testament is the same as the Jewish scriptures, for example.

They might think that Hindu devotion to God or Muslim belief in giving to charity are good examples for Christians to follow and **might think that all religions have something to learn from each other**.

In some cities, members of different religious groups meet together for discussions and prayer to encourage different members of the community to live peacefully together.

Test yourself

1 Why do some Christians think that other world religions are wrong?

2 What do missionaries do?

3 Explain why other Christians are happy to meet together with members of different faith communities.

Check the facts

One of the most important facts to remember about Christianity is that Jesus was not a Christian but a Jew.

A Christian is someone who follows the teachings of Jesus Christ and no one called themselves a Christian until some time after Jesus' final ascension into heaven.

Jesus was born in Judaea, which was ruled by the Roman Empire but was still a Jewish country with Jerusalem as its holy city. **He was brought up in a Jewish home and would have followed the laws of the Torah**. He would have attended the synagogue in Nazareth several times a week and visited Jerusalem with his parents to celebrate the three great Jewish festivals of Pesach, Shavuot and Sukkot. **Jesus' disciples were also Jews**, as were most of the people to whom he preached.

Many of Jesus' teachings are based on the Torah, and he said:

> 'Do not think that I have come to abolish the Law or the Prophets; I have not come to abolish them but to fulfil them.'
> (Matthew 5:17)

Like John the Baptist, Jesus was trying to bring people back to living according to God's rules. It is not clear whether Jesus thought he was the Messiah who the Jews were waiting for, but many of his followers did believe this.

Even after Jesus' resurrection, his disciples continued to pray in the Temple and it was some time before Christianity became a separate religion.

Test yourself

1 How important is it to remember that Jesus was a Jew?

2 What did Jesus' followers mean when they said he was the Messiah?

3 What is a Christian?

Check the facts

Some people argue that there must be a God because there must have been something which started off the whole universe. This is known as the cosmological argument for the existence of God.

People say that the universe could not have just started itself. Everything happens for a reason, because of something else which made it happen. There must have been something that started the universe off, and this must have been God.

People also say that the world looks as though it has been very carefully designed. This is known as the teleological argument for the existence of God.

They say that the careful balance of gases that make up the atmosphere, the way in which the eye works just like a camera, or the beautiful patterns on a butterfly or a seashell, show the existence of a God who plans and designs things. The world could not have developed features like these by itself. There must be someone who designed them and created them, which is God.

Some people say that because we know what is right and wrong, this means that there must be a God who tells us through our consciences about what we should and should not do. This is known as the moral argument.

Test yourself

1 Explain in your own words:
a) the cosmological argument
b) the teleological argument
c) the moral argument

for the existence of God.

2 Do you think that any of these arguments is convincing? Give reasons for your answer.

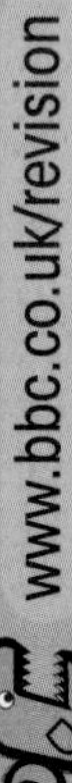

Check the facts

Religious experiences are when people feel that they have contact with something that is to do with God, rather than with the physical world in which they live. People may have many different types of religious experience.

Visions

Many people believe that they have seen visions of heaven and the saints. Some people, such as **Joan of Arc, Saint Theresa** and **Saint Bernadette** have seen visions of angels or of the Virgin Mary, who have spoken to them and guided them in their lives. Even today, people sometimes say that they see visions, particularly of Mary.

Miracles

A miracle is something that happens and that goes against the normal physical laws of the world. A miracle might be when someone is cured of a disease or sickness after medical techniques have failed, or when someone survives a disaster when there is no logical explanation for this.

Numinous

This is sometimes called the '**holy other**'. Sometimes, when people go into a particular building or a particular place, they have a feeling that there is something different or special and holy about it.

Another type of religious experience is an event such as the **Toronto Blessing**, when many people have a particular experience of God and believe that they are filled with the Holy Spirit and must go and tell other people so that they can share in this.

Test yourself

1 What is a religious experience?

2 Discuss two types of religious experience.

3 People often say that miracles no longer happen. What do you think about this?

Check the facts

Most Christians believe that one of the ways in which God works in the world is through miracles.

Usually, a miracle is understood to be something that is unexpected and goes against the laws of nature, done by God for a special reason. In the Old Testament, some of the most famous miracle stories are:

- The parting of the Red Sea (Exodus 14)
- Manna in the wilderness (Exodus 16)
- The fall of Jericho (Joshua 6)
- Daniel is saved from the lions (Daniel 6)

In the New Testament, Jesus is shown as performing miracles, for example:

- Jesus calms a storm (Matthew 8:23)
- The feeding of the five thousand (Luke 9)
- The raising of Jairus' daughter (Luke 8)
- Jesus turns water into wine (John 2)

In the Bible, miracles are seen as proof of God's involvement in the world and control over the events of history. **In the New Testament, miracles are also seen as a proof that Jesus really was from God.**

Some people believe that the miracle stories of the Bible are not meant to be taken literally; they say that it is impossible for modern people to believe in them. They say that the stories were written long ago by people who did not have a great understanding of science. But most Christians believe that miracles are important, that God can do the impossible, and that miracles still happen today.

Some Christians hold healing services, where people who are ill or disabled can go in the hope of a miraculous cure. Some Christians go on pilgrimages to places such as Lourdes, where they hope that miracles will occur.

Test yourself

1 What sort of event might be called a miracle?

2 Give two examples of miracles from the Old Testament and two examples from the New Testament.

3 What are the miracle stories of the Bible meant to show about God?

4 Where might Christians go today if they hope for a miraculous cure for illness or disability?

Check the facts

The Bible is the most important and holy book in Christianity.

Because Christians believe that the Bible is the 'word of God', they try to understand its messages and to put them into practice in their daily lives.

Reading the Bible

- The Bible is read in every church service, and often a **sermon** is given that explains the meaning of some of the passages.
- Many Christians read the Bible on their own at home, or in small groups, as well as hear it read in church.

Is the Bible 'true'?

Some Christians believe that the Bible is literally true. This means that they think that everything in the Bible happened in exactly the way that it is described. These Christians are often called '**fundamentalists**' or '**creationists**'.

Other Christians believe that parts of the Bible are not literally true, but are true in other ways, perhaps as myths, hymns or poems. They believe that sometimes, the Bible displays an understanding of the world that is outdated now. For example, they might think that the Bible's attitude to women is not appropriate for the modern world, and they might think that scientists have a better understanding than the Biblical writers of the origins of the world.

These Christians might have difficulties in knowing which parts of the Bible are myth, and which parts really are true.

Test yourself

1. Explain why Christians try to do what the Bible says.
2. Explain why Christians might have different opinions about whether the Bible is literally true.
3. Give two examples of times when Christians might read the Bible, or hear the Bible being read.

Check the facts

The Christian Bible is divided into two sections. These are usually called the Old Testament and the New Testament.

There are also some other books that you might find in some versions of the Bible. These are called **Apocryphal books** and are usually found between the Old Testament and the New Testament.

The Old Testament

The Old Testament contains 39 books that together make up the whole of the **Jewish Bible – the Tenakh**. Jews refer to the first five books of their scriptures:

Genesis, Exodus, Leviticus, Numbers, Deuteronomy

as the **Torah (Law)** and they believe that these books were given to Moses by God. The books of the Old Testament contain different types of writing: Law, Prophecy, Poetry, and History.

The New Testament

The New Testament is the writings of some of the first Christians. The individual books were not brought together until 367 CE. In the New Testament there are 27 books.

- The first four books are the **Gospels**. These are called:

after the people who were said to have written them. **The Gospels are about the main events in the life of Jesus, although not much is known about him before he was baptised by John the Baptist and became a preacher.**

The word 'Gospel' means 'good news' –

The Gospel is the good news that Jesus was the Son of God who had come to Earth to save people from sin.

- The next book is the **Acts of the Apostles**. This is sometimes said to be the second part of Luke's gospel. The Acts begins with the **ascension of Jesus** – when he finally went up to heaven after the **resurrection**, and gives an account of the first years of the Christian church.
- The next 21 books are called the **Epistles**, or letters. Two are said to have been written by **Peter** and another three by **John**. Many of the others were written by the apostle **Paul**. **These men were the earliest leaders of the Christian church**, and they wrote to places where there were small communities of believers to give them encouragement and guidance. Many Christians still find help and guidance from the Epistles today.
- The final book of the New Testament is called the **Apocalypse** or **Book of Revelation** and is a book of prophecy about what will happen on the last days of the world.

Test yourself

1 What are the Jewish Scriptures called?

2 What does the word 'Gospel' mean.

3 What are the Epistles, and why are they so important?

The Ten Commandments

Check the facts

The Ten Commandments are ten rules that Jews and Christians believe were made by God and given to Moses to pass on to everyone else. They are part of the 'covenant', or agreement, made between God and humanity.

The Ten Commandments are found in several places in the Old Testament, including Exodus 20. **Jews and Christians believe that these rules apply to everyone all the time, and give an outline of the right way to live.**

The Ten Commandments are:

1. You shall have no other gods.
2. You shall not worship idols.
3. You shall not misuse the name of God.
4. Remember the Sabbath day and keep it holy.
5. Honour your father and mother.
6. You shall not murder.
7. You shall not commit adultery.
8. You shall not steal.
9. You shall not give false testimony against your neighbour.
10. You shall not covet (be envious of) your neighbour's possessions.

The first four commandments are about how people should behave towards God. The other six are about how people should treat each other.

Test yourself

1 What is another word for 'covenant'?

2 Which of the following are from the Ten Commandments:
a) Love your neighbour as yourself
b) Honour your father and mother
c) An eye for an eye, a tooth for a tooth
d) Love your enemies and pray for your persecutors?

3 Give examples of:
a) two Commandments which are about the right relationship between people and God
b) two Commandments which are about how people should behave towards each other.

4 Explain why Jews and Christians think that the Ten Commandments are so important.

The Sermon on the Mount

Check the facts

During his ministry, Jesus spent much of his time in and around **Galilee**, where he preached and performed miracles. Jesus often taught in **parables** about the Kingdom of God and about forgiveness. He delivered a sermon, usually called the **Sermon on the Mount**, when he was near to the Sea of Galilee (Matthew 5–7). During this sermon he taught people the **Beatitudes** and the **Lord's Prayer**:

The beatitudes:
Blessed are the poor in spirit,
for theirs is the kingdom of heaven.
Blessed are those who mourn,
for they will be comforted.
Blessed are the meek,
for they will inherit the Earth.
Blessed are those who hunger and thirst for righteousness,
for they will be filled.
Blessed are the merciful,
for they will be shown mercy.
Blessed are the pure in heart,
for they will see God.
Blessed are the peacemakers,
for they will be called sons of God.
Blessed are those who are persecuted because of righteousness,
for theirs is the kingdom of heaven.

Blessed are you when people insult you, persecute you and falsely say all kinds of evil against you because of me. Rejoice and be glad, because great is your reward in heaven, for in the same way they persecuted the prophets who were before you.
(Matthew 5:3–12)

In these teachings, Jesus was explaining to his listeners that although they often had to suffer in their lives on Earth, God loved them and they would be rewarded and comforted when they died and went to heaven.

The Lord's Prayer

Jesus said that often people made a great fuss about praying and prayed in public so that other people would see them and see how holy they were. He said that this was wrong and told people that they should pray using the **Lord's Prayer**.

Our Father in heaven, hallowed be your name,
your kingdom come, your will be done
on Earth as it is in heaven.
Give us today our daily bread.
Forgive us our debts, as we also have forgiven our debtors.
And lead us not into temptation, but deliver us from the evil one.'
(Matthew 6:9-13)

This is now one of the best known of all Christian prayers and is used in every church service as well as by people praying at home.

The Sermon on the Mount also contains other important teachings:

- Jesus taught people not to judge others:

'Do not judge, or you too will be judged. For in the same way as you judge others, you will be judged, and with the measure you use, it will be measured to you. (Matthew 7:1-2)

- He taught that adultery and divorce were wrong:

It has been said, 'Anyone who divorces his wife must give her a certificate of divorce.' But I tell you that anyone who divorces his wife, except for marital unfaithfulness, causes her to become an adulteress, and anyone who marries the divorced woman commits adultery. (Matthew 5:31-32)

- He also taught that people should forgive others:

You have heard that it was said, 'Love your neighbour and hate your enemy.' But I tell you: Love your enemies and pray for those who persecute you, that you may be sons of your Father in heaven. (Matthew 5:43-45)

Test yourself

1 Where did Jesus spend much of his time preaching?

2 Who did Jesus say would be called 'the children of God'?

3 Why is the Lord's Prayer so important?

4 How should Christians treat their enemies according to the Sermon on the Mount?

The Good Samaritan

Check the facts

The Good Samaritan is a parable told by Jesus. The Parable of the Good Samaritan can be found in Luke's Gospel, 10:25–37.

A parable is a story that is told to teach a message.

The story uses the sorts of people and situations that are familiar to the listeners or readers, in order to illustrate a point and make it more lively and memorable. Jesus, like other Jewish teachers, often taught in parables.

In New Testament times, Samaritans were disliked because they were descended from mixed-race, mixed-religion marriages. Other Jews thought that they were impure and inferior.

All of the Gospel writers showed that Jesus cared for everyone equally, but Luke especially chose to emphasise this part of Jesus' teaching.

Jesus told the parable as an answer to someone who asked 'Who is my neighbour?' He wanted to know what it meant to 'Love your neighbour as yourself', and which people this applied to. The parable tells the story of a Jew who was travelling from Jerusalem to Jericho when he was attacked and robbed. A priest and a Levite, both well-respected members of Jewish society, saw him lying injured but did nothing to help. A passing Samaritan also saw the injured man and helped him to an inn, where he paid for the man to stay until he felt better. Jesus told this story to illustrate the point that all people have a duty to treat each other as 'neighbours', even when they are strangers or from different ethnic backgrounds.

Christians believe that the message of this parable is to show that it is the character of the person that matters, not the outward appearance. Everyone should be treated as a neighbour, and an equal, and should not be disregarded because of prejudices.

Test yourself

1 What does the word 'parable' mean?

2 Give two other examples of parables told by Jesus.

3 Explain how a Christian today might use this parable in a discussion about racism.

Check the facts

In Matthew's gospel, Jesus describes what will happen on the Day of Judgement. He says:

> 'When the Son of Man comes in his glory, and all the angels with him, he will sit on his throne in heavenly glory. All the nations will be gathered before him, and he will separate the people one from another as a shepherd separates the Sheep from the Goats. He will put the Sheep on his right and the Goats on his left.

The Sheep are seen as the good people and the Goats as the bad. The King, God, says to the Sheep:

> 'Come, you who are blessed by my Father; take your inheritance, the kingdom prepared for you since the creation of the world. For I was hungry and you gave me something to eat, I was thirsty and you gave me something to drink, I was a stranger and you invited me in, I needed clothes and you clothed me, I was sick and you looked after me, I was in prison and you came to visit me.' 'Then the righteous will answer him, 'Lord, when did we see you hungry and feed you, or thirsty and give you something to drink? When did we see you a stranger and invite you in, or needing clothes and clothe you? When did we see you sick or in prison and go to visit you?'

God explains that what people do for each other, they also do for him:

> 'The King will reply, 'I tell you the truth, whatever you did for one of the least of these brothers of mine, you did for me.'

In this parable, Jesus is preparing his followers for the end of time when all people will be judged by God according to the way they have lived their lives. **The importance of the teaching is that Christians should always look after those who are less fortunate than themselves as this is what God wants.**

Test yourself

1 According to this parable, who are the Sheep and who are the Goats?

2 What are the five things that good people should do according to this parable?

3 Why do you think this is such an important parable in Christian teaching?

What is abortion?

Check the facts

An abortion is when a pregnancy ends before a baby is born. If this happens naturally, it is called a 'spontaneous abortion' or a 'miscarriage'. If it happens because of a deliberate choice, it is called a 'procured abortion'.

There are many reasons why a woman might consider having an abortion:

- because her health would suffer if the pregnancy continues
- because the foetus is not developing normally
- because she is pregnant as a result of contraceptive failure
- because her relationship with the father has ended
- because the pregnancy is a result of rape
- because she is very young and still in full-time education
- because she just does not want to have a baby.

Some people think that none of these is a good reason for having an abortion. Other people think that they are all good reasons, and others think that only some of the reasons justify abortion.

Abortion and the law

Abortion was against the law in the UK until the **1967 Abortion Act**. Before then, if women wanted to end their pregnancies, they had to go secretly to someone who would perform an illegal, or **'back-street' abortion**.

In **1990**, the issue was debated again. **It is legal to have an abortion if two doctors agree that the health of the mother or her existing children would be harmed if the pregnancy continued, or if the foetus is seriously abnormal.**

The law allows abortions only up to the 24th week of pregnancy, unless the mother's life is at risk. **24 weeks is when the foetus becomes viable which means that it could survive on its own outside the womb**. By law, medical staff do not have to take part in carrying out abortions, or caring for women who have had abortions.

Test yourself

1 What is meant by:
a) procured abortion b) 'back-street' abortion c) viable?

2 Under what circumstances is an abortion legal in the UK?

3 Under what circumstances, if any, do you think that an abortion is justifiable? Give reasons for your answer.

Check the facts

The Roman Catholic Church has very strict views about abortion. These views are based on the Bible and on church teachings.

The Roman Catholic Church teaches that God created life and therefore only God can take it away. It says that a human being receives its soul at the moment of conception – the point when the egg is fertilised by the sperm. Therefore, any form of contraception involves killing a human life and so abortion is seen as murder. Two important biblical teachings that are used in this discussion are:

> Before I formed you in the womb I knew you. (Jeremiah 1:5)

> For you created my inmost being; you knit me together in my mother's womb. (Psalm 139:13)

Both of these teachings suggest that God is aware of the new human life as a person whilst the foetus is still in the womb. Therefore, the foetus is a living person before it is born and must be treated with the same respect as any other human being.

The doctrine of 'double effect'

There is only one condition on which an abortion may take place. If it is essential for the mother to have an operation, not an abortion, and the effect of that operation is that the foetus will unavoidably die, then this is permitted. This is called the **doctrine of 'double effect'**. An example would be an ectopic pregnancy. The mother has become pregnant but instead of the foetus being in the womb it is in the fallopian tubes. If nothing is done then both the baby and the mother will die, therefore the operation needs to be performed even though it will cause an abortion.

Test yourself

1 a) What does the Roman Catholic Church teach about abortion?
b) What reasons does it give for its views?

2 What biblical teachings might Roman Catholics use to support their views on abortion?

3 What is meant by 'the doctrine of double effect'?

22 Other denominations' views about abortion

Check the facts

None of the Christian churches encourages abortion, and there are Christians of all denominations who believe that abortion is always wrong.

Some Christian churches, such as the **Anglican Church (Church of England)**, the **Methodists**, and the **URC (United Reformed Church)**, teach that abortion can sometimes be the best solution to a problem, particularly in serious cases, such as:

- when the mother is very young
- if her health would be at risk if she had the baby
- there is a high risk that the baby would have some kind of abnormality.

Many Christian churches teach that decisions about abortion are a matter for the individual's conscience. These churches teach that forgiveness and compassion are important, as well as the sanctity of life, and that Christians should not be too quick to condemn others. They teach that decisions about abortion are never easy and that different situations might need different responses.

Like the Roman Catholics, other denominations also recommend that young people should be given adequate sex education, and that single mothers should receive support from the church.

Test yourself

1 Give two examples of Christian denominations that teach that abortion might, in some circumstances, be the best decision.

2 a) What does it mean to say that decisions about abortion are a matter for the individual conscience?
b) How does this differ from the teaching of the Roman Catholic Church?

Check the facts

Euthanasia is 'painless killing to relieve suffering'. The word comes from two Greek words, 'eu' which means 'good', and 'thanatos' which means 'death'.

There have been many debates about euthanasia. Some Christians argue that it is kinder and, so, an example of **agape (Christian love)** to allow, or help, someone to die if they are suffering and nothing will relieve it.

• Euthanasia can be **voluntary**. Some people refer to voluntary euthanasia as **assisted suicide**. Someone might, for example, have an incurable illness or condition that is causing them so much pain that they do not want to live.

• Euthanasia can also be **involuntary**. A doctor might feel that a patient's life should end. They might be in **PVS (Persistent Vegetative State)** where they are completely unconscious and unaware of the world about them and there is no hope for recovery.

• **Active euthanasia** is when some positive step is taken to bring on death. This could be a massive dose of pain killers or other drugs, for example.

• **Passive euthanasia** is when no action is taken which would be necessary if the person were to be kept alive, and so he or she is allowed to die.

Euthanasia and the law

In most countries, it is against the law for a doctor or anyone else to assist in any form of euthanasia. However, a doctor or a patient might choose to stop treating an illness, so that death can come more quickly, or, in order to reduce the pain, a doctor might have no choice but to prescribe a very high dose of painkillers and, as a result, the patient will die.

Some people actively campaign for voluntary euthanasia to be made legal, while others are opposed to the legalisation of euthanasia because they fear it would lead to involuntary euthanasia becoming common practice for old people, or because they believe that it breaks the Commandment:

You shall not murder (Exodus 20:13)

Test yourself

What is meant by:

1 voluntary euthanasia **2** involuntary euthanasia
3 active euthanasia **4** passive euthanasia

Check the facts

Roman Catholics believe that every human life is made 'in the image of God' (Genesis 1:27). This means that there is something special about humanity that makes people different from all other kinds of animal. They believe that God came into the world in the form of a man, and that this shows that humanity has a special relationship with God which cannot be destroyed.

The Roman Catholic Church teaches that it is always wrong to take away human life deliberately, even if the motive is good. The only time euthanasia can be allowed is if death occurs as a side-effect of something that was intended to help the patient, for example if the dose of a drug to control pain needs to be so high that the patient's life is shortened as a result. This is known as **the law of 'double effect'**.

Roman Catholics do not believe that life must be forced to continue under all circumstances. Ordinary treatments must be carried out, but it is not necessary to give 'extraordinary' treatments which have very little chance of success and which might cause distress to the patient or the family.

Suffering and pain

Roman Catholics believe that suffering can sometimes bring people closer to God, because it helps them to share in the sufferings of Christ. They believe that God sometimes uses pain as a way of teaching people. Pope John Paul II, in a statement called **Evangelium Vitae (1995)**, wrote of the need for **'a positive understanding of the mystery of suffering'**. They also believe that suffering helps people to treat each other better, as they learn about patience, courage and compassion.

Many Roman Catholics support the work of **hospices**, as places which provide care for the dying. They believe that this is a good alternative to euthanasia.

Test yourself

1 Why do Roman Catholics believe that euthanasia is wrong?

2 Why do Roman Catholics believe that suffering can sometimes have positive effects?

3 What do Roman Catholics mean by the term 'double effect'?

Other denominations' views about euthanasia

Check the facts

Although most Christian denominations are not in favour of euthanasia, not all of them have the same views about it as the Roman Catholic church.

The **Church of England** teaches that life is a gift from God and that Christians must offer protection and care to those who are very ill or dying. It teaches that it would be wrong for a doctor to help someone to die but that there is no obligation to prolong life by every possible means, especially if this would prolong suffering. The Church believes that the hospice movement is a positive alternative to allow people to spend their last days and die with dignity.

The **Russian Orthodox Church** believes that euthanasia is wrong but that individuals have the right to refuse painful and unnecessary treatment. However, patients should make this decision with their doctors, family and priest. The Church also believes that sometimes it is right to pray for someone's death so that their suffering can be relieved.

The **Methodist Church** is considering the use of a **Living Will** – a document signed by the person concerned, which says that if they are ill, with no real hope of recovery, they do not wish to be kept alive at all costs, and that only pain relieving treatment should be given. However, these Living Wills do not, as yet, have any legal status in Britain.

Quakers make a distinction between allowing someone to die and **mercy killing**. Some support the Hospice movement, whilst others believe that those in great pain should have the option of choosing death rather than continuing to live with suffering.

Test yourself

1 What is a 'Living Will'?

2 Explain why the Russian Orthodox Church believes that sometimes it is right to pray for a person's death.

3 In what circumstances do some of the Churches believe that people should be allowed to die?

The hospice movement

Check the facts

Hospices, as places of shelter, have been around for hundreds of years, but the modern hospice movement was begun in Dublin at the end of the nineteenth century, by a group of nuns who wanted to provide care for people who were dying and had no family to look after them.

St Joseph's Hospice was set up in London in 1967 by Cicely Saunders, who was then a young nurse. She was inspired by a Polish man who was dying in a busy hospital ward in London without any family around him. She used to visit him regularly, and he left her some money to open her hospice. Cicely Saunders believes that adequate pain relief is the key to a peaceful death, and that many people would not consider euthanasia if they were confident that they would not die in pain.

What hospices do

- provide care for people who are terminally ill, and also for their families.
- They try to make death as peaceful and painless as possible.
- They give medical treatments, such as pain-relieving medicines, and give help in other ways, such as providing counselling for the patients and families.
- They also offer respite care, which is for people who are usually looked after at home, to give the people who care for them a break and the chance to have a rest or go on holiday.
- Some hospices are especially for children.
- Many hospices depend on voluntary workers, fund-raising and donations.

Some Christians support the work of hospices as an alternative to euthanasia, and as a way of putting their Christian beliefs into practice. They believe that care for the dying is important, and that it is better to have a peaceful natural death than to encourage death to come more quickly.

Test yourself

1 Who founded St Joseph's Hospice, and when?

2 Explain the main aims of hospices.

3 Why might a Christian choose to support a hospice, rather than supporting the right to choose euthanasia?

Roman Catholic and other views about contraception

Check the facts

The Roman Catholic Church teaches that all human beings share in God's creation and that sexual relationships must only take place within marriage.

- The **Roman Catholic Church** teaches that a marriage should be 'unitive', bring the couple close together, and 'procreative'. **Therefore, when a married couple have sexual intercourse this should always have the possibility of leading to new life and the woman becoming pregnant.** It teaches that this is **in accordance with Natural Law and God's intentions**.

Any artificial means where the woman is prevented from becoming pregnant are seen as going against one of the purposes of marriage, and are therefore wrong. Artificial means include the use of **the pill, the coil, condoms** and the **'morning after' pill**. The Church also says that **sterilisation** of either the man or the woman, in order to prevent them from being able to be parents, is wrong.

The only form of contraception that is available for Catholics is the **'rhythm method'**. In this technique, the couple only have intercourse at those times of the month when the woman is unlikely to become pregnant. However, Catholics are also expected to take responsibility for family planning, provide for their children and not put undue strain on the marriage.

However, the Church does say that necessary treatment for a medical condition that results in the woman being unable to become pregnant is acceptable.

- The **Church of England** believes that contraception is a means of allowing a couple to enjoy sex together whilst also taking responsibility for their family.
- The **Quakers** teach that decisions about contraception should be left up to the couples concerned and some feel that they have a duty to limit the size of their families to help control the expansion in world population and also to allow the woman to play a greater part in society.

Test yourself

1 What does the Roman Catholic church teach about the purposes of marriage?

2 What form of family planning are Roman Catholics allowed to use?

Christian views about fertility treatment

Check the facts

Fertility treatment is medical help given to people who want to have babies but are unable to conceive naturally. Usually this is because of medical problems, but sometimes it is because the person who wants the baby is single, or in a gay relationship, or past the natural age for child-bearing. Often, fertility treatment is not available on the National Health, and people have to pay for it.

There are several different fertility treatments available, and they do not always work.

- **AID** is **Artificial Insemination by Donor**, when sperm is donated by an anonymous man.
- **AIH** is **Artificial Insemination by Husband**, when the egg and the sperm come from the couple who want to be parents, but medical help is needed for fertilisation to take place.
- Sometimes, women who don't ovulate normally receive **donor eggs** from another woman. Some women receive medication to encourage them to ovulate.
- **IVF** is **In Vitro Fertilisation**, where the egg and sperm are brought together for fertilisation in a laboratory rather than inside the woman's body. If embryos form, some or all of them are implanted in the woman's uterus in the hope that a successful pregnancy will result.

The Bible and fertility treatment

The Bible does not say anything about fertility treatment because it was written before any of these techniques were possible. But there are stories about people who are desperate because they cannot have children, and who are helped by God, for example, Hannah, who eventually gave birth to the prophet Samuel (1 Samuel 1:1–20).

Different views

- Some Christians believe that fertility treatment is wrong because it interferes with nature and with God's plan for that couple. They might say that if a couple cannot conceive naturally, this is because God does not want them to become parents.
- Other Christians believe that fertility treatment is often a good thing because it helps to bring new life into the world and gives happiness to the people who want to be parents.

Objections to fertility treatment

Christians often express reservations about some aspects of fertility treatments, even if they believe that, on the whole, they are a good thing:

- They might object to the **creation of 'spare embryos'** during IVF, which are sometimes destroyed or use for medical research. They might argue that an embryo is still a human life, and should be protected.
- They might object to the **use of eggs or sperm from anonymous donors** because this introduces a third adult into the family relationships, and some think that this is similar to adultery.
- They might object to **fertility treatments being made available for people who are not married, or who are homosexual or past the age for child-bearing**, because they might see this as unnatural and not the way God intended things to happen.

Christians believe that life is sacred, and that this should be respected whenever decisions are made about the beginnings of human life.

Test yourself

1 Briefly explain some of the different kinds of fertility treatment available.

2 What do Christians mean when they say that life is sacred?

3 Why might some Christians object to fertility treatments that use eggs or sperm from anonymous donors?

4 Why might some Christians object to fertility treatments that create 'spare' embryos?

Check the facts

Christian aid agencies work across the world to try and relieve the suffering of those who are in poverty, suffering from the effects of natural disasters, such as droughts, and who are disadvantaged.

These agencies base their work on Biblical teachings, such as:

'and if you spend yourselves on behalf of the hungry and satisfy the needs of the oppressed, then your light will rise in the darkness, and your night will become like the noonday.' (Isaiah 58:10)

the commandments of Jesus: 'Love the Lord your God with all your heart and with all your soul and with all your mind and with all your strength . . . Love your neighbour as yourself.' (Mark 12:30–31)

Three of the main Christian aid agencies are:

Christian Aid

Christian Aid
We believe in life before death

This organisation represents more than forty denominations in the United Kingdom and Ireland. Christian Aid came into existence as '**Christian Reconstruction in Europe**' after the Second World War to help those who were suffering as a result of the fighting. Later, the name of the organisation was changed to Christian Aid and it began to work worldwide. It now works in over seventy countries on a huge variety of projects.

Christian Aid not only deals with emergencies and disasters when they happen, but also works to try to prevent crises and to improve people's lives by giving them skills and education so that they do not have to depend on outside help and aid. Much of Christian Aid's money is raised during Christian Aid Week, which is held each year in May.

Caritas

Caritas is a Roman Catholic aid organisation that works in over 150 countries. Caritas works with all people, not just Catholics. As well as giving people support in times of need, it develops social projects so that people can be enabled to 'take personal charge of their own lives and destiny, and thus achieve that liberty which is their inalienable right as children of God.'

CAFOD

CAFOD represents Caritas in England and Wales. It now funds over 1000 projects in the Developing World.

Tearfund

Tearfund is the **Evangelical Relief Fund** and was founded in 1968 to help the famine victims of the civil war in Nigeria. It has an annual income of over £20 million.

In the same way as Caritas and Christian Aid, Tearfund believes that people should not just be given aid and charity during disasters, but that agencies should work to help people to become skilled and self-sufficient so that they can take care of themselves.

As well as the Christian aid agencies, there are also other charities such as **OXFAM** which have similar aims but which are not religious organisations.

Test yourself

1 What teachings is the work of Christian aid agencies based on?

2 Name three Christian aid organisations.

3 Each of these agencies believes that it should do more than just provide food and aid during disasters. Explain what other help they try to give.

The use of wealth

Check the facts

The Bible teaches that 'the love of money is the root of all evil.' (1 Timothy 6:10).

Jesus taught that people who focus their lives on making money will find it impossible to love God too. Jesus expected his followers to give to the poor because they were Jews and charity is part of the Jewish law.

According to Jesus, in order to serve God, rich people should sell their possessions and give the money to the poor.

The proper use of money

Different Christians have different opinions about the right uses of money.

- Some believe that Jesus was not exaggerating when he said that, in order to love God, you must give all your money to the poor.
- Monks and nuns take vows of poverty and give up all their possessions to live in communities where they devote themselves to prayer and to the service to others.
- Some believe that it is wrong to have church buildings full of treasures, or churches that own a lot of land, when there are people in the world who are starving.
- Others say that a beautiful church is a way of showing devotion to God and that it helps people to worship.

Helping the poor

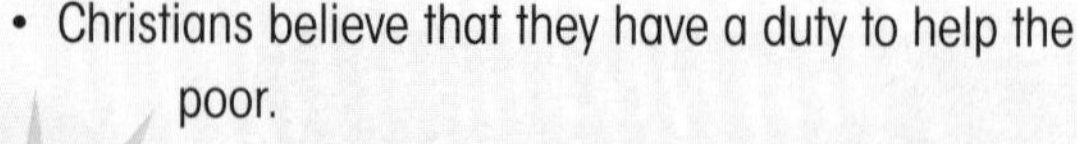

- Christians believe that they have a duty to help the poor.
- The Bible teaches that care for the poor and the weak is one of the most important aspects of loving God.

Examples of Biblical teaching about care for the poor include:

- Whoever loves God must also love his brother. (1 John 4:21)

- So in everything, do to others what you would have them do to you. (Matthew 7:12)

Test yourself

1 What did Jesus mean when he talked about a servant with two masters?

2 Why do Christians disagree about whether churches should own land and treasures?

3 Complete the following Biblical quotations:
   a) Whoever loves God must also . . .
   b) Whatever you did for one of the least of these brothers . . .
   c) So in everything do to others . . .
   d) The love of money . .

The work of Mother Teresa

Check the facts

Mother Teresa of Calcutta was born Agnes Gonxha Bojaxhiu in Shkup, Albania, on 27 August 1910. She died in Calcutta on 5 September 1997.

1928 – she went to Ireland where she joined the **Order of the Sisters of Our Lady of Loreto**. Six weeks later she sailed to India where she worked as a teacher. Soon she asked if she could work, instead, with the many poor people of Calcutta. She studied nursing and then moved into the slum area where she received permission to set up a hostel.

1948 – she established the **Order of the Missionaries of Charity**, she took Indian citizenship and her nuns all changed their traditional habits for saris.

1950 – The order was approved by the Pope and has been subject only to the Pope's rulings since **1965**. In addition to the three basic vows of poverty, chastity and obedience, nuns of her order take a fourth vow pledging service to the poor.

1952 – she opened the **Nirmal Hriday ('Pure Heart') Home for Dying Destitutes** in Calcutta. She opened centres across India serving the blind, the elderly, lepers, cripples, and those who were dying. The Order also established a leper colony near Anansol called **Shanti Nagar (Town of Peace)**. Mother Teresa continued as head of the order until her retirement in March **1997**.

1963 – the Indian government awarded her the **Padmashri ('Lord of the Lotus')** for her work with the people of India.

1971 – On 6 January, Pope Paul awarded her the first **Pope John XXIII Peace Prize**.

1979 – she was awarded the **Nobel Prize for Peace**.

By the end of the twentieth century the Missionaries of Charity had more than 1000 nuns with sixty centres in Calcutta and more than 200 across the world.

Test yourself

1 Give an outline Mother Teresa's life.

2 What is the name of the Order of nuns which Mother Teresa founded?

3 What are the four vows that nuns of the Missionaries of Charity take?

Check the facts

During the second half of the twentieth century, people became much more aware that the environment was being damaged by modern lifestyles. Many different problems have been caused, including:

- **Pollution** – domestic rubbish and industrial waste are difficult to get rid of and can poison wildlife and clog rivers and streams. Chemical spillages at sea have caused considerable damage to animals and plants. Poisonous gases formed during industrial processes get into the water cycle and cause acid rain. Traffic fumes pollute the air that we breathe.
- **Global warming** – an increase in the production of carbon dioxide and other gases has led to climate changes, which cause floods, storms and hurricanes, and upset the delicate balance of gases in the Earth's atmosphere.
- **Using up the world's natural resources** – the Earth's supply of resources, such as coal, gas and oil, is rapidly being used up. These are non-renewable resources, which means that once they have been used, they cannot be replaced.
- **Destruction of natural habitats** – people have destroyed huge areas of the world's rainforests, seas and hedgerows, making it very difficult for many species to survive in the world.

Some of the ways in which Christians and other people can help the environment include using 'green' products, such as cleaner fuel; recycling paper, glass etc; reducing how much electricity, gas and coal they use; voting for parliamentary candidates who promise to deal with environmental issues; campaigning on local issues, such as the destruction of hedgerows; using public transport and car sharing or cycling to work; reducing the amount of rubbish they produce or joining an organisation that campaigns on behalf of the environment.

Greenpeace, the **Worldwide Fund for Nature**, and **Friends of the Earth** are all examples of organisations Christians might choose to support. Many such organisations are not Christian, but Christians support them because the work they do fits in with their beliefs that the world is God's creation.

Test yourself

1. Explain what is meant by a) pollution; b) deforestation; c)non-renewable resources; d) global warming.
2. Make a list of six different things that Christians could do to try and protect the environment.

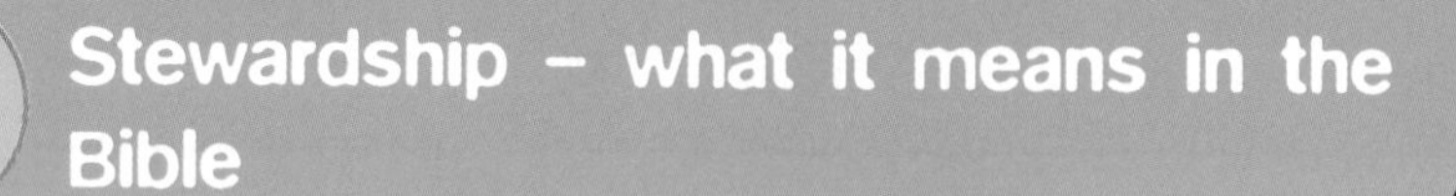

33 Stewardship – what it means in the Bible

Check the facts

A steward is someone who looks after something for someone else. The dictionary says a steward is 'an official who controls the domestic affairs of a household, etc.'

In the Bible, the idea of stewardship appears in Genesis:

> Then God said, 'Let us make man in our image, in our likeness, and let them rule over the fish of the sea and the birds of the air, over the livestock, over all the Earth, and over all the creatures that move along the ground.' So God created man in his own image, in the image of God he created him; male and female he created them. God blessed them and said to them, 'Be fruitful and increase in number; fill the Earth and subdue it. Rule over the fish of the sea and the birds of the air and over every living creature that moves on the ground.'
> (Genesis 1:26-28)

In this passage, God gives humans the task of looking after the Earth and all the life on it: plants, animals and the balance of the environment. Due to these teachings, Christians believe they have a duty to care for the world.

Ideas of stewardship

The **Church of England** says that it is the responsibility of all people to do everything they can to prevent pollution, ensure the world's resources are available equally to all people, and prevent damage to plants and animals.

The **Roman Catholic** church believes that all people should respect, care for and share the Earth's resources.

In the eighteenth century, a **Quaker**, John Woolman, said, 'The produce of the Earth is a gift from our gracious creator to the inhabitants and to impoverish the Earth now to support outward greatness appears to be an injury to the succeeding age.'

Test yourself

1 What is meant by the word 'steward'?

2 Explain the biblical teachings that might be used when discussing stewardship.

3 What do the Roman Catholic church and the Quakers teach about stewardship?

Check the facts

Christians believe that humans are set apart from other animals because humans have souls whereas animals do not. Christians do not believe that animals have equal status and equal rights with humans.

The book of Genesis teaches that humanity has a special role in the world: to rule over the other species:

> Then God said, 'Let us make man in our image, in our likeness, and let them rule over the fish of the sea and the birds of the air, over the livestock, over all the Earth, and over all the creatures that move along the ground.' (Genesis 1:26)

Most Christians believe that animals do not have the same rights as humans. Most Christians eat meat, for example, and in the Bible, Jesus helped the fishermen to catch more fish to eat. **Many Christians believe that using animals for medical research is acceptable**, as long as the animals are not caused any more suffering than is necessary.

Christians believe that they have a responsibility to act as stewards of the Earth and the species within it. **They believe that they should take care of the animals and respect them because they are part of God's creation** and they have been given the job of caring for the world. **They do not agree with anything that causes animals unnecessary suffering**.

Test yourself

1 Why do Christians think that animals do not have the same status as people?

2 What might a Christian say about:
- a) fox hunting
- b) wearing fur
- c) eating meat
- d) testing drugs on animals?

3 Explain why Christians believe that they should respect other animals.

Racism and apartheid

Check the facts

Racism is putting into practice beliefs about discrimination. Some people think that others are different and inferior to them because of their race or the colour of their skin. Some people say that racism equals prejudice plus power.

There are often items in the news about racism. In the United Kingdom this racism often comes from white people. It is usually directed towards black (Afro-Caribbean) people, Asians and Chinese. These people become the victims of racism because of the colour of their skin or because of their religious beliefs. Because, in the United Kingdom, white people are in the majority, they have the power to put this prejudice into action.

The apartheid laws

Although racism can be found all over the world, one of the most extreme forms was the **apartheid laws** of the **Republic of South Africa**.

The term apartheid means 'separateness' in Afrikaans, the language of some of the white people who live in South Africa.

Apartheid was the name given to the laws that led to the **segregation** of the population of the country according to whether they were white, black or coloured (Indian and mixed race). These laws were first introduced in South Africa in **1948** and meant that people of different races:

- had to live in different towns and parts of the country
- could only hold some particular jobs
- were not allowed into certain shops, hospitals and public places.

Apartheid laws finally came to an end in February **1990** at the same time as the black leader, **Nelson Mandela**, was released from prison. The first non-racial elections were held in South Africa in **1994**, when all people were allowed to vote, regardless of colour or race.

Test yourself

1 What is meant by 'racism'?

2 Why do you think that some people are racist?

3 Explain apartheid and the effect it had on the lives of people in South Africa.

Biblical teaching about racism and equality

Check the facts

The Bible teaches that all people are made 'in the image of God' (Genesis 1:27). For Christians, this means that all people share something of the nature of God.

The Bible emphasises that those who love God should treat foreigners as if they were brothers. They should pay foreigners the same wages that they pay everyone else, welcome them into the community, treat them fairly and look after them if they are in trouble. The Bible often calls foreigners 'aliens', which means strangers from another place.

When an alien lives with you in your land, do not ill-treat him. The alien living with you must be treated as one of your native-born. (Leviticus 19:33)

Christians are taught that their faith unites them, so they should not look for differences between one person and another:

There is neither Jew nor Greek, slave nor free, male nor female, for you are all one in Christ Jesus. (Galatians 3:28)

Christians are taught that it is wrong to discriminate between people because of their appearance:

My brothers, as believers in our glorious Lord Jesus Christ, don't show favouritism. (James 2:1)

Test yourself

1 What does the Bible mean when it refers to 'aliens'?

2 Complete the following quotations from the Bible:
a) My brothers, as believers in our glorious Lord Jesus Christ. . .
b) There is neither Jew nor Greek. . . for you are all one. . .
c) When an alien lives with you in your land, do not. . . The alien living with you must be treated as. . .

Martin Luther King Jr. and Trevor Huddleston

Check the facts

Martin Luther King Jr. and Trevor Huddleston are two well-known Christians who have fought against racism.

Martin Luther King Jr.

1929 – Martin Luther King Jr. was born on 15 January in Atlanta, Georgia, the son of a Baptist minister. He studied at Morehouse College and was ordained as a Baptist minister when he was eighteen. He was influenced by the works of Mahatma Gandhi and this led him to follow Gandhi's teaching of non-violence and peaceful protest.

1954 – he became pastor of the Dexter Avenue Baptist Church in Montgomery, Alabama. Although the Supreme Court of America had banned all racial segregation in schools, there was still a lot of racism in the southern states of America.

1955 – Dr King was asked to lead a bus boycott in Montgomery. This was to protest about racial segregation, after a black woman, Rosa Parks, had refused to give up her seat to a white passenger. The protest lasted for 381 days, during which time Dr King was arrested and put in gaol, his home was bombed, and threats were made against his life. The boycott ended in **1956** when the Supreme Court made such segregation illegal.

Dr King was made President of the Southern Christian Leadership Conference and in **1960** became co-pastor, with his father, of the Ebenezer Baptist Church in Atlanta. He now played a very active part in the growing **civil rights** movement.

1963 – on **28 August, in Washington D.C., Martin Luther King made his most famous speech** in which he said:

> 'I have a dream that one day on the red hills of Georgia the sons of former slaves and the sons of former slave owners will be able to sit down together at the table of brotherhood.
>
> I have a dream that my four little children will one day live in a nation where they will not be judged by the color of their skin but by the content of their character.'

1964 – Dr King was awarded the **Nobel Peace Prize**.

1968 – on 4 April 3, Martin Luther King was shot and killed in Memphis, Tennessee. Some 100 000 people went to his funeral in Atlanta.

1983 – the third Monday in January was proclaimed a national holiday in America in honour of Martin Luther King Jr.'s birthday.

Trevor Huddleston

1913 – Trevor Huddleston was born, in England. He became an Anglican priest in **1937** and joined the Community of the Resurrection (Mirfield Borthers).

1943 – he went to South Africa and was in charge of missions in Vrededorp (Sophiatown) and Orlando. He was head of the order from **1949** to **1953**.

1953 – the South African government moved the black people of Vrededorp to create an all-white area. Trevor Huddleston supported the black population against the government and became **Chairman of the Western Areas Protest Committee**.

1956 – he was forced to leave South Africa by the government.

He wrote several books about the black struggle against apartheid and became famous all over the world for his opposition to the South African government.

1960–1968 – Trevor was **Bishop of Masasi in Tanzania**

1968–1978 – he was **Suffragan Bishop of Stepney in London**

1978–1983 – he was **Archbishop of the Indian Ocean**

From 1983 – he was **chairman of the International Defence and Aid Fund for Southern Africa**

1969–1981 – he was **Vice-President of the Anti-Apartheid Movement**

1995 – he finally returned to South Africa, and received a knighthood in **1998**, just before his death, for his work against injustice in South Africa and the world.

1998 – Trevor Huddleston died.

Test yourself

1 Why do you think people like Martin Luther King Jr. and Trevor Huddleston devote their whole life to causes like racism?

2 What biblical teachings might support them in their work?

Check the facts

The Bible teaches that God made the two different sexes so that they could join together in marriage as a life-long partnership.

Christians believe that when a man and a woman are joined together in marriage, this is a symbol of the love Christ has for the Church.

Christians believe that marriage exists so that two people can be together as partners, and so that children can be brought into the world in the context of a loving family.

The Roman Catholic Church teaches that marriage is a sacrament, which is a symbol of the grace of God. According to Roman Catholic beliefs, a marriage that has been made by God in church cannot be undone.

In a Christian marriage service:

- the couple begin by making a statement to the rest of the congregation saying that they are **free to marry**.
- Each partner is asked to **give consent** to the marriage, to show that they are marrying of their own free choice.
- The couple **make vows** to each other and exchange rings. In the vows, the bride and groom promise to love, honour and comfort each other. They promise to be faithful to each other for the rest of their lives.
- The minister **declares that the couple are husband and wife**, and says that what God has joined together, humanity should not separate.
- The couple **sign the register** to show that the marriage is legal, and usually there is a reception or a party after the service.

Test yourself

1 What is the purpose of marriage, according to Christianity?

2 Explain what Roman Catholics mean when they say that marriage is a sacrament.

3 What do the bride and groom promise each other in their wedding vows?

4 For how long do Christians expect a married couple to stay committed to each other?

Roman Catholic and other views about marriage after divorce

Check the facts

The Christian churches have different views about divorce but most of them agree that it can only be a last resort for a couple who are married.

The vows of the marriage ceremony are made to God, and the Bible teaches that marriage is a life-long commitment.

The **Roman Catholic church does not allow divorce**. If a marriage has completely failed it may be possible for the couple to receive an annulment but this can only be granted under certain conditions:

- the marriage was not consummated
- one of the people being married did not understand the significance of marriage
- in certain circumstances where the woman is unable to have children.

An annulment means that the original marriage never took place and so the couple are free to remarry in the church. If a Roman Catholic couple just have a civil divorce they cannot remarry in the church.

The **Church of England recognises that sometimes divorce is the only option** available for people, but it has not yet decided whether divorced people should be allowed to remarry in church.

Most other denominations do now permit remarriage after divorce if the new couple can show that they are truly committed to one another. However, although divorce may be inevitable and the only possible way forward for the people concerned, it is always viewed as regrettable and as a last resort.

Test yourself

1 Why is divorce always seen only as a last resort?

2 What is an annulment?

3 Explain two different Christian views about divorce and remarriage.

Check the facts

Christians believe that getting married and having children is important but not compulsory. Some people choose to stay single and to follow their faith in other ways. Jesus never married.

One of the Ten Commandments is about family life:

> Honour your father and mother. (Exodus 20:12)

The Bible teaches that Christians have a duty to care for their relatives:

> If anyone does not provide for his relatives, and especially for his immediate family, he has denied the faith and is worse than an unbeliever (1 Timothy 5:8)

Christians believe that the family has an important role to play in religious life. It is the place where children first learn about their religion and about love, tolerance and forgiveness. In a Christian family, children learn about their parents' faith and how it affects their lives; and also about Christian festivals and what it means to be part of a church community.

Families are often in the best position in the local community to give hospitality to strangers, to adopt or foster children, and to care for the elderly. **Christians believe that love should not just be for family members, but that everyone should be treated as if they were brothers and sisters.**

The **Mothers' Union** is a Christian organisation devoted to supporting family life. Its members try to help families in many ways, such as providing child care for single parents, helping the families of people who are in prison, and giving people who care for elderly or disabled relatives a break.

Test yourself

1 True or false?

a) The Mothers' Union is only open to mothers.

b) Christians believe that everyone has a duty to marry and have children.

c) 'Honour your father and mother' is one of the Ten Commandments.

d) Christians believe that you should always put your own family first.

2 What does the Bible say about people who do not care for their relatives?

3 What do Christians believe that children gain from being brought up in a Christian family?

Check the facts

Both the Old and New Testaments stress that elderly people and relatives should be cared for:

> 'Honour your father and your mother, so that you may live long in the land the Lord your God is giving you. (Exodus 20:12)
>
> If anyone does not provide for his relatives, and especially for his immediate family, he has denied the faith and is worse than an unbeliever. (1 Timothy 5:8)

Christianity teaches that elderly people have already contributed a great deal to the world and to their families and therefore they should be shown respect. They should not be forgotten simply because they have become ill or frail and are no longer able to work or, perhaps, look after themselves.

Many Christians put these teachings into practice in their own families and also by working with old people who are their neighbours or are members of their church community. Others may contribute towards the work of organisations such as **Age Concern** or **Help the Aged**.

Help the Aged

This is a charity that provides practical support to help older people live independent lives, particularly those who are frail, isolated or poor. As well as providing practical help, the charity also acts as a pressure group on the government to improve pensions and care for the elderly and to fight ageism at work and elsewhere.

Age Concern

Age Concern is a charity that is committed to improving living conditions for elderly people by influencing the government and local authorities to improve people's lives.

Test yourself

1 What does the Bible say about caring for elderly people and relatives?

2 Explain how a charity might work to help improve the life of elderly people.

Christian attitudes towards sex and sexuality

Check the facts

Christianity teaches that the sexual relationship between a man and a woman is a gift from God that should give them both pleasure and can lead to the gift of children for the couple.

Because of this teaching, Christians believe that the only place for sexual relationships is in marriage. The Prayer Book of the Church of England says:

> A wedding is one of life's great moments, a time of solemn commitment as well as good wishes, feasting and joy. St John tells us how Jesus shared in such an occasion at Cana, and gave there a sign of new beginnings as he turned water into wine. Marriage is intended by God to be a creative relationship, as his blessing enables husband and wife to love and support each other in good times and in bad, and to share in the care and upbringing of children. For Christians, marriage is also an invitation to share life together in the spirit of Jesus Christ. It is based upon a solemn, public and life-long covenant between a man and a woman, declared and celebrated in the presence of God and before witnesses.

For these reasons, sexual relationships outside of marriage are not accepted by any of the Christian denominations.

Homosexual relationships

All of the churches have found homosexual relationships a difficult area to accept because they do not meet the requirements of marriage. The Church of England accepts that some people are homosexual, but suggests that although they should be welcomed in church, they should not take part in physical acts of love. The only denomination that has fully accepted same-sex relationships is the Religious Society of Friends (Quakers).

Test yourself

1 Why do Christians believe that sexual relationships should only take place within a marriage?

2 Explain different Christian attitudes towards homosexuality.

Check the facts

The Bible says nothing about smoking and taking illegal drugs because these were not issues when the Bible was written. But drinking alcohol is mentioned in the Bible quite often and it is seen as a normal part of life. **Many Christians believe that drinking alcohol is acceptable as long as it is done sensibly and moderately.**

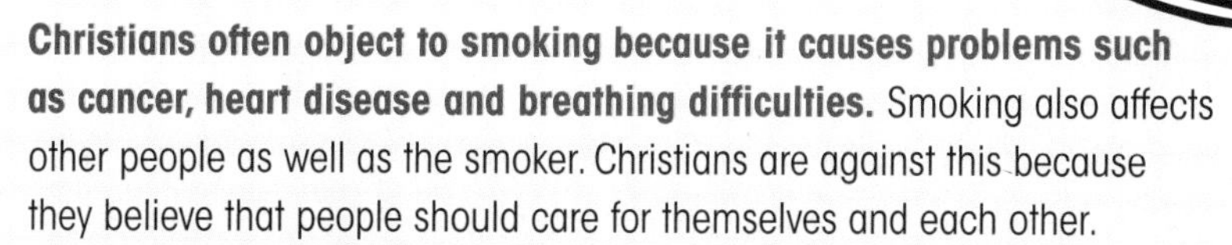

Christians often object to smoking because it causes problems such as cancer, heart disease and breathing difficulties. Smoking also affects other people as well as the smoker. Christians are against this because they believe that people should care for themselves and each other.

Taking illegal drugs and drinking too much alcohol cause serious health problems and can make people behave badly. Christians believe that it is important to exercise self-control.

Smoking, drugs and alcohol are all expensive, addictive and can cause family problems. In a letter to a new church, Paul explained that Christians should have respect for their own bodies because the Holy Spirit lives in them:

> Don't you know that you yourselves are God's temple and that God's Spirit lives in you?

Some churches, such as the Salvation Army and the Methodists, encourage their members not to drink alcohol at all, so that they can set a good example when they work with the homeless and people with drink problems. When these churches celebrate Holy Communion, they use non-alcoholic wine out of respect for people who never drink.

Test yourself

1 Complete this Biblical quotation:

> Don't you know that you yourselves are God's . . . and that God's Spirit . . . ?

2 Give five reasons why Christians might object to smoking, drugs and alcohol.

3 Name two Christians churches that encourage their members not to drink alcohol at all.

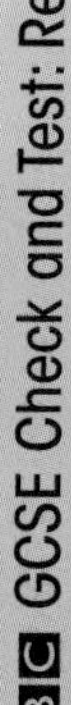

Care for the disabled

Check the facts

Christians believe that they have a duty to help the weak. Jesus showed concern for people who were blind, who were paralysed or had leprosy, and Christians try to follow his example by showing the same concern themselves.

Some Christians support organisations, such as Mencap, which help people with learning disabilities and their families. Mencap:

- provides services, such as special accommodation and education
- educates the public about the needs of those with learning disabilities
- campaigns to influence the government when it is making decisions that affect their lives.

Leonard Cheshire and **Sue Ryder** are two Christians who, because of their Christian faith, devoted their lives to helping the disabled. They realised that people in wheelchairs and those who were elderly or ill and could not manage to look after themselves independently, needed somewhere to live where they could be cared for while still having as much independence and privacy as possible. There are now Leonard Cheshire homes and Sue Ryder homes all around the country, and in other parts of the world too.

Christians care for people with disabilities since they believe that all people are made '**in the image of God**'. In the Sermon on the Mount, Jesus taught:

> 'In everything, do to others what you would have them do to you' (Matthew 7:12)

Christians believe that this means that they should treat the disabled in the way that they would like to be treated if they had the same disabilities.

Test yourself

1 Give two reasons why Christians believe that they should help people with difficulties.

2 Briefly explain the work of Mencap.

3 Name two people who have set up homes for people who cannot cope independently.

4 Give an example of Biblical teaching that Christians might use to show that they should care for the disabled.

Homelessness and the work of the Salvation Army

Check the facts

The Salvation Army was set up in England in 1865 as the 'Christian Mission'. Its founder was a Methodist minister, William Booth.

It follows Jesus' teachings in the Parable of the Sheep and the Goats when he said:

> 'For I was hungry and you gave me something to eat, I was thirsty and you gave me something to drink, I was a stranger and you invited me in, I needed clothes and you clothed me, I was sick and you looked after me, I was in prison and you came to visit me.' (Matthew 25:35–36)

The original aim of the Army was to spread the Christian Faith and to help the poorest people of London. **It changed its name to the Salvation Army in 1878 and William Booth took the title of General.**

After the Second World War, the Salvation Army helped by providing soup kitchens and shelter for the homeless as well as trying to prevent crime amongst young people. **Today, the Salvation Army works in over one hundred countries and has more than three million members.** It provides schools, maternity homes and children's homes as well as still providing hostels with free lodging and free meals. The Army runs:

- more than 800 hostels for the homeless (35 000 people are helped each year)
- 152 homes and centres for alcoholics and people with drug problems
- 18 institutes for the blind
- 30 homes for the physically handicapped
- 250 canteens
- 780 homes for the elderly
- 352 hospitals
- 200 children's homes
- 1400 schools
- 130 centres for refugees
- 106 remand homes
- 78 student homes.

Although the Salvation Army is a Christian organisation and charity, it offers help to everyone, regardless of race or religion.

Test yourself

1 What biblical teaching supports the work of the Salvation Army?

2 Why was the Salvation Army founded?

3 Explain how the Salvation Army works to help homeless people.

Check the facts

Christians believe that suicide is wrong because it shows a lack of trust in God and it involves destroying the life that God gave. It also causes a great deal of hurt for the people left behind.

In the past, suicide was treated as a crime. Anyone who tried and failed to commit suicide was severely punished, and if someone did succeed in committing suicide, they were not allowed to be buried in the churchyard with everyone else. Suicide used to be treated as a form of murder.

Today, most people recognise that people attempt suicide when they are very unhappy, rather than because they are bad people. People have a much better understanding of mental illness now than they had a hundred years ago. Suicide is different from self-sacrifice, when people give up their own lives because they know it will help others.

Young men are more likely to commit suicide than women, and the suicide rate has risen quite dramatically during the past fifty years.

The Samaritans is an organisation that was set up to try to prevent suicide. It was started by a vicar called **Chad Varah** but it is not only for Christians. Its volunteers and the people it helps do not have to be Christians. The Samaritans offer counselling by telephone, e-mail or face-to-face, for people who are thinking of committing suicide. They encourage callers to talk through their problems and try to think of alternative ways of solving them. The Samaritans is staffed by volunteers.

Test yourself

1 How have attitudes to suicide changed over the last hundred years?

2 Why do Christians think that suicide is wrong?

3 Why might a Christian support an organisation such as the Samaritans?

4 Explain briefly the work done by the Samaritans.

Are men and women equal?

Check the facts

While most people today might accept that men and women are equal and should be treated equally, the churches have often appeared to believe that, in some ways, women were inferior to men.

In the Old Testament, Eve picks the apple of the Tree of the Knowledge of Good and Evil, which God told her not to do, and is blamed for Adam and herself being thrown out of the Garden of Eden.

In the New Testament, Paul says:

> 'Women should remain silent in the churches. They are not allowed to speak, but must be in submission, as the Law says. If they want to enquire about something, they should ask their own husbands at home; for it is disgraceful for a woman to speak in the church.' (1 Corinthians 14:34–35)

However, in his letter to the Galatians he says that men and women are equal:

> 'There is neither Jew nor Greek, slave nor free, male nor female, for you are all one in Christ Jesus.' (Galatians 3:28)

It seems that the Bible has different ideas about whether men and women are equal. Until recently, the churches have not allowed women to become priests or ministers, but this has changed, and **now only the Roman Catholic and Orthodox churches still insist that priests must be men.**

The Roman Catholic church says that 'Each of the two sexes is an image of the power and tenderness of God, with equal dignity though in a different way.' (Catechism of the Catholic Church paragraph 2335)

Test yourself

1. Explain what the Bible says about the equality of men and women.
2. Why do you think that some churches do not allow women to become priests or ministers?
3. Explain Roman Catholic teaching about the equality of men and women.

Women in the Church

Check the facts

Christians have different views about the right role for women in the Church. The ordination of women (making women priests) is one of the issues that most sharply divides Christians, and is a major obstacle to Christian unity.

Some churches, such as the Roman Catholic Church and the Eastern Orthodox Church, believe that women should not be ordained as priests. They believe that the priest represents Christ when Holy Communion is celebrated, and that it would not be appropriate for a woman to take on this role.

They sometimes argue that God came into the world as a man, not a woman, and that Jesus chose men, not women, for his disciples, and that it was Peter, not a woman, who was chosen to be the founder of the Christian Church. This might be taken to show that Christian priesthood is for men, and that women have different roles that are also important.

Other churches, such as the Salvation Army and the United Reformed Church, have always had women in their leadership as equals with men. They do not believe that there is any problem with women being ordained, as long as they are suitable as individuals and are entering the ministry for the right reasons. They believe that men and women were created as equals and that women have special qualities to bring to Christian leadership.

The **Church of England** had long debates about the ordination of women. **It did not have women in its leadership until 1994, when the first Anglican women priests were ordained.** Some people were very unhappy about this and left the Church of England because of it.

Test yourself

1 Give two examples of Christian churches that have always had women in the ministry.

2 Give two examples of Christian churches that believe that women should not be ordained as priests.

3 When did the Church of England first ordain women as priests?

4 For what reasons do some people think that it is not appropriate for women to be priests?

Check the facts

According to Christian teaching, war is something that should always be avoided. However, sometimes war may seem inevitable.

All war is an attempt by one group or power to defend itself against another or to try to take something, which may be as basic as freedom, from another group. A **Just War** is seen as a war that has to be fought but is conducted according to certain conditions. These conditions were first proposed by **Thomas Aquinas (c. 1225–74)** and **Francisco de Vitoria (1483-1546)** and are still used by Christians today.

The conditions of a Just War are:
- it must be fought by a legal, recognised authority, such as a government
- the cause of the war must be just
- the war must be fought with the intention to establish good or correct evil
- there must be a reasonable chance of success
- the war must be the last resort (after all diplomatic negotiations, and so on, have been tried and failed)
- only sufficient force must be used and civilians must not be involved.

These conditions are designed to prevent war and to limit its effects.

Some wars can meet all of these conditions. For example, **World War II (1939–1945)** would appear to have been a Just War because:
- it was fought by Germany and the Allied countries, who were legal authorities
- Germany was being attacked for invading other countries
- the intention was to correct the evil that Germany was doing
- the Allies felt that they had a reasonable chance of success, and won
- all forms of negotiation with Hitler and the Third Reich had failed
- most of the fighting was limited to the armies concerned and to harbours and munitions sites.

Test yourself

1 What are the conditions for a Just War?

2 Look at some of the wars which are happening today and decide whether they meet the conditions of a Just War.

Check the facts

The Bible does not have a single consistent view about war and violence. Different parts of the Bible were written in different historical contexts. Some were written when Israel was a successful nation, some were written when the people were in exile. Others, such as much of the New Testament, were written when the Romans occupied the country and Christians feared for their lives.

In some parts of the Bible, people are encouraged to go and fight, as part of God's plan for history:

> No one will be able to stand up against you;
> you will destroy them.
> (Deuteronomy 7:24)

> Proclaim this among the nations; prepare for war! (Joel 3:9)

One of the very oldest pieces of writing in the Bible is a song about victory in war:

> The Lord is a warrior;
> The Lord is his name.
> Pharaoh's chariots and his army
> He has hurled into the sea . . .
> (Exodus 15:3–4)

In the New Testament, Jesus once became violent when he saw how people were misusing the Temple:

> He overturned the tables of the money-changers
> and the benches of those selling doves.
> (Mark 11:15)

In other parts of the Bible, there are teachings which suggest that it is never right to use violence or to go war:

> Blessed are the peacemakers.
> (Matthew 5:9)

Love your enemies, and pray for those who persecute you.
(Matthew 5:44)

'Put your sword back in its place,' Jesus said to him, 'for all who draw the sword will die by the sword.'
(Matthew 26:52)

The Bible gives different teachings about war and violence, and Christians have different opinions about it, all of which can usually be supported by reference to the Bible.

Test yourself

1 What reasons might there be for the fact that the Bible gives different advice about war and violence?

2 Give an example of a time when Jesus used violence.

3 Give two examples of Biblical teaching that might be used to support fighting in a war, and two which might be used to argue against fighting.

Christians and pacifism

Check the facts

Many people say that Christianity is a pacifist religion, which does not approve of fighting and warfare.

Sometimes it is said that this is based on Biblical teaching. Although the Sixth Commandment says 'You shall not murder' (Exodus 20:13), there are several occasions when the Jews are told by God to attack people who oppose them. The famous expression 'But if there is serious injury, you are to take life for life, eye for eye, tooth for tooth, hand for hand, foot for foot.' (Exodus 21:23–24) was intended to limit revenge, not to encourage it.

Jesus is often described as a pacifist. He taught 'Blessed are the peacemakers for they will be called the children of God' (Matthew 5.9).

However, there are occasions in the gospels when Jesus is obviously angry:

One of these is in the Temple in Jerusalem:

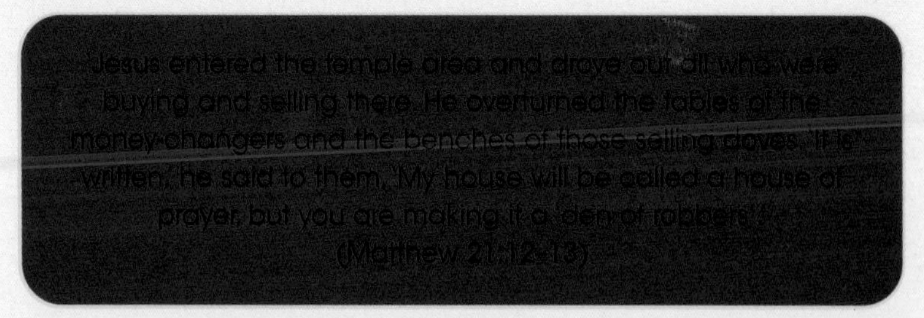

Jesus entered the temple area and drove out all who were buying and selling there. He overturned the tables of the money-changers and the benches of those selling doves. 'It is written,' he said to them, 'My house will be called a house of prayer, but you are making it a 'den of robbers'.'
(Matthew 21:12–13)

Most Christians believe war and fighting are wrong except in the most severe cases. They base their views on Jesus' teaching about love:

> ''A new command I give you: Love one another.
> As I have loved you, so you must love one another.'
> (John 13:34)

Some Christians, such as Quakers, are totally opposed to fighting and during warfare they are 'conscientious objectors'. They are prepared to go into battle driving ambulances or doing other duties, but they will not fight. Other Christians are prepared to fight in the armed services and there are always chaplains attached to military units.

Test yourself

1 Do you agree that Jesus was a pacifist?

2 Explain how a Quaker might behave during a war, and why.

Check the facts

Most people use non-violent protest when they want to make a point. Many problems can be sorted out by discussion, letter, negotiation, law courts and the use of the vote, especially in places where there's democracy and freedom of speech. **When people talk about non-violent protest, they usually mean extreme situations where people live with injustice.**

People use non-violent protest when they believe that violence is wrong, or that it will not be as successful as other methods of protest. Methods of non-violent protest include:

- sit-ins
- marches and public demonstrations
- fasting and hunger striking
- non-payment of taxes
- letter-writing and advertising
- public speeches
- symbolic actions, such as chaining to railings or trees
- boycotts.

Mahatma Gandhi was not a Christian but he was famous for using non-violent methods of protesting against British rule in India.

Martin Luther King was a Christian who famously insisted that supporters of the **Civil Rights Movement** in the USA should use only non-violent methods of protest against the unfair treatment of black people. He gave speeches and organised boycotts, marches and sit-ins to make his point that black people should have equal rights with white people. He was a Christian and believed that retaliating with violence was wrong.

Both Gandhi and Martin Luther King died violently. They were shot by assassins.

Some people believe that using violence would reduce them to the level of the people against whom they are protesting. They hope that, through peaceful demonstrations, they will be able to gain respect for their ideas. **Other people think that violence is sometimes the only solution.** Liberation theologians, animal rights activists and others sometimes think that violence is the only way in which they are going to be able to defend the weak effectively.

Test yourself

1 What were (a) Gandhi and (b) Martin Luther King protesting about?

2 What methods did they use?

3 Which one of them was a Christian?

4 Why do some people think that non-violent protest is always preferable to using violence?

5 Why do others disagree?

Human rights and prisoners of conscience, Amnesty International

Check the facts

Amnesty International was founded by Peter Benenson, a British lawyer, in 1961. It is committed to promoting all human rights as found in the Universal Declaration of Human Rights.

Amnesty campaigns:

'to free all prisoners of conscience; ensure fair and prompt trials for political prisoners; abolish the death penalty, torture and other cruel treatment of prisoners; end political killings and "disappearances"; and oppose human rights abuses by opposition groups.'

Amnesty has over a million members in more than 160 countries.

Amnesty International works by setting up campaigns of **letter-writing, publicity and protests** so that people may become aware of particular human rights abuses. It believes that many countries who practise these abuses do not wish the rest of the world to know what is going on and so may stop if they are exposed.

Amnesty is best known for its work in individual cases, but it also aims to change laws and policies to protect people. It has campaigned against **torture** and for **the abolition of the death penalty**. In **1988** it worked to set up an international court that has been joined by 120 countries. This exists to bring those guilty of human rights abuses to trial.

Although Amnesty is not a Christian organisation, many Christians support its work because, by doing so, they are expressing their belief in the value of human life and showing **agape**(see page 10).

Test yourself

1 What are the aims of Amnesty International?

2 How does Amnesty carry out its work?

3 Explain why a Christian might decide to join Amnesty International.

Check the facts

Liberation theology began in the 1960s in Central and South America, mainly within the Roman Catholic Church. The movement believes that Christians have a duty to stand up and fight against poverty, oppression and injustice.

Liberation theologians believe Christians should take positive action when they see abuses of human rights. They should take sides with the poor and speak out against unjust governments.

Some followers of liberation theology have become involved in violent struggles with governments in order to defend the weak. **In Columbia, Father Camilo Torres became a fighter and was killed in a battle against government forces.** In some countries, the government has organised the killing of priests and other Christian leaders who stand up for human rights.

Some people disagree with liberation theology, saying that it is wrong for Christians to become too much involved with politics, and wrong for them to use violence even to defend the weak.

The message of liberation theology has spread to other countries outside Central and South America. It has influenced many Christians who work with the poor in the inner cities, and those who have been involved in movements, such as the struggle against apartheid in South Africa.

Test yourself

1 Where did liberation theology begin?

2 Why have some Christian priests been involved in armed battles against governments?

3 For what reasons do some people disagree with liberation theology?

4 How has liberation theology influenced people in other countries?

Biblical teaching about crime and punishment

Check the facts

The Bible has quite strict rules about crime and punishment. In the Old Testament, the Ten Commandments give a set of rules that the Israelites were required to obey, which include:

- 'Six days you shall labour and do all your work, but the seventh day is a Sabbath to the Lord your God. On it you shall not do any work, neither you, nor your son or daughter, nor your manservant or maidservant, nor your animals, nor the alien within your gates.'
- 'You shall not murder.'
- 'You shall not commit adultery.'
- 'You shall not steal.'
- 'You shall not give false testimony against your neighbour.'
- 'You shall not covet . . .'

(Exodus 20: 9-10, 13-17)

When a man is found gathering wood for a fire on the Sabbath, Moses asks God what to do and is told to put him to death for breaking the Commandment. However, there are also many examples of God forgiving people for breaking the laws in the Old Testament. The Old Testament also limits the amount of punishment which can be given:

> Show no pity: life for life, eye for eye, tooth for tooth, hand for hand, foot for foot.
> (Deuteronomy 19:21)

This seems to suggest that people should be punished by losing what they have taken from someone else. However, the passage is actually limiting revenge: you cannot take more than a tooth for a tooth. At the time this was written, it probably meant a payment to the value of a tooth or a hand.

In the New Testament, Jesus speaks about forgiveness for wrongdoing:

> Then Peter came to Jesus and asked, 'Lord, how many times shall I forgive my brother when he sins against me? Up to seven times?' Jesus answered, 'I tell you, not seven times, but seventy-seven times.'
> (Matthew 18:21–22)

When Jesus is nailed to the cross, he still offers forgiveness to the people who have put him there:

> Jesus said, 'Father, forgive them, for they do not know what they are doing.'
> (Luke 23:34)

Paul also says in his letter to the Romans:

> Do not repay anyone evil for evil.
> (Romans 12:17)

Test yourself

1 Explain what the Old Testament says about forgiveness and punishment.

2 What does 'an eye for an eye' mean?

3 What did Jesus teach about forgiveness for crimes?

Check the facts

Christianity teaches that God is loving and forgiving and that Christians should try to love and forgive everyone, even their enemies. But this does not mean that criminals should be allowed to get away with breaking the law.

Christians believe that there are four main reasons why people should be punished when they commit crimes:

1 Deterrence – punishment is meant to put other people off committing the same crime themselves.

2 Retribution – this is another word for revenge. If a criminal hurts someone, a lot of people think that he or she should be paid back for the crime by being made to suffer.

3 Protection – some punishments, such as imprisonment or the death penalty, stop the criminal from doing any more harm. The punishment protects the rest of society from the criminal.

4 Reformation – the punishment should help the offender to become a better person. The person who has committed the crime should learn from his or her mistakes, and understand why the crime was wrong.

Working with criminals

Some Christians have devoted time to working with criminals and trying to help them to turn away from crime. For example, **Elizabeth Fry** was a member of the **Religious Society of Friends (Quakers)** in the eighteenth century. She devoted her life to improving conditions for prisoners, making sure they had proper food, some privacy and the chance to learn a trade, so they would be less likely to go back to crime when they were released.

Some Christians belong to organisations such as the **Howard League for Penal Reform**, which aims to improve conditions for prisoners. Others help prisoners by visiting them regularly and giving them gifts at Christmas, or by running activities, such as drama groups and choirs, in prisons.

Test yourself

1 Name an organisation that works to improve conditions in prisons.

2 Which parable includes visiting people in prison as an example of how Christians should help others?

3 Explain the four main purposes of punishment.

4 What did Elizabeth Fry do to help people in prison?

Check the facts

Although all the Christian churches would agree that it is wrong to kill people, they have different views about capital punishment.

> The Church of England believes that the justice system must by merciful but should also show that wrongdoing will be punished. The General Synod of the Church said recently that any reintroduction of capital punishment would be 'deplored'.

The Roman Catholic Church has never said officially that capital punishment is wrong, although many bishops have made statements condemning it. The church allows that capital punishment may be necessary in some extreme circumstances. However, the bishops of the church believe that the death penalty should not be allowed because:

- it undermines the respect for human life
- mistakes can be made in the justice system and so innocent people might be executed
- most people who have been executed come from poor and underprivileged backgrounds and this should be taken into account. Steps should be taken to help them rather than punish them by execution.

The Religious Society of Friends (Quakers) has always been totally opposed to capital punishment:

> A deep reverence for human life is worth more than a thousand executions in the prevention of murder; and is, in fact, the great security for human life. The law of capital punishment while pretending to support this reverence, does in fact tend to destroy it.
> (John Bright MP, 1868)

Test yourself

1 What is meant by capital punishment?

2 Explain the Quaker view of capital punishment.

3 What do the Roman Catholic bishops say about capital punishment?

Why do people suffer?

Check the facts

The problem of evil is one of the most difficult questions for Christians. If God can do anything, and God is perfectly loving, why does he allow people to suffer? Why does God not stop evil and suffering whenever it is about to happen? Why did God make people if he knew that they would behave badly?

The **Book of Job** in the Old Testament gives one approach to the subject. It tells the story of a man who suffers a great deal because he is being tested by God. He loses his home, his family, his wealth and his health, but still he continues to praise God and keeps to his faith. Eventually, Job demands to talk to God directly to find out why he has been made to suffer so badly. God shows Job all the wonders of creation and demonstrates that he is God. **Job realises that in comparison with God he is very small, and that he cannot expect to understand what God does; he must just accept it.**

Some ideas on suffering

Two famous Christians in the early history of the Church produced their own ideas about why people suffer:

Irenaeus said that we meet evil and suffering in our lives so that we can grow and develop in a relationship with God. If we never suffered and were always programmed to do the right thing, we would never learn anything or be able to make any important choices. Irenaeus believed that suffering is part of God's plan.

Augustine did not believe that God meant suffering to happen. He taught that God created the world to be perfect. But the first people, Adam and Eve, disobeyed God. This is known as the **Fall**. The Fall was so important that it affected the whole of creation.

Christians have different ideas about why we suffer, and many accept that we do not know all the answers. Because Christians believe in life after death, this often comforts them when they suffer because they believe that everything will be put right in heaven.

Test yourself

1 What is meant by 'the problem of evil'?

2 Explain the main message of the book of Job.

3 What are the main differences between the views of Irenaeus and the views of Augustine? Do you agree with either of these views?

Check the facts

People sometimes say that God and the Devil are opposites. God represents everything that is good and the Devil represents everything that is bad.

The Bible does not say very much about the Devil or Satan. There are stories from outside the Bible that explain that the Devil was once an angel called Lucifer. He tried to be as important as God and because of this sin he was thrown out of heaven. God sent Lucifer to rule over hell for ever. One of the few Bible references about the Devil is found in Luke's gospel where Jesus is talking about the Devil:

> He replied, 'I saw Satan fall like lightning from heaven.'
> (Luke 10:18)

Christianity teaches that it is the Devil who tempts people to do wrong and to go against the love and wishes of God. **The Devil tempted Jesus during his forty days in the wilderness, but Jesus was able to resist all his temptations.**

Christians believe that there is a force for evil as well as a force for good, but **in the modern world, many people find it hard to believe that there is such a being as the Devil and they may, instead, believe that this power that tempts people to do the wrong thing is within each person.**

Test yourself

1 Who was Lucifer?

2 When did Jesus encounter the Devil?

3 Explain what Christians today might believe about the Devil.

Check the facts

The story of the creation of the world is found in Genesis:

'In the beginning God created the heavens and the Earth. Now the Earth was formless and empty, darkness was over the surface of the deep, and the Spirit of God was hovering over the waters. And God said, 'Let there be light,' and there was light. God saw that the light was good, and he separated the light from the darkness. God called the light 'day', and the darkness he called 'night'. And there was evening, and there was morning – the first day.'
(Genesis 1:1–5)

On the **second day** God created the **oceans and the sky.**

On the **third day**, the **land and the plants**.

On the **fourth day the sun, moon and stars.**

On the **fifth day** God created **everything that lives in the sea and also the birds.**

On the **sixth day** God created **the animals and men and women.**

'Let us make man in our image, in our likeness, and let them rule over the fish of the sea and the birds of the air, over the livestock, over all the Earth, and over all the creatures that move along the ground.' So God created man in his own image, in the image of God he created him; male and female he created them. God blessed them and said to them, 'Be fruitful and increase in number; fill the Earth and subdue it. Rule over the fish of the sea and the birds of the air and over every living creature that moves on the ground.'
(Genesis 1:27-28)

On the **seventh day the creation was complete and God rested.**

Test yourself

1 What is the order of creation?

2 What was different about the creation of human beings?

3 What was special about the seventh day?

Scientific theories about the origins of the universe and of humanity

Check the facts

The study of the origins of the universe is known as cosmology.

Scientists believe that the universe began with a massive explosion called the **Big Bang**. This sent matter and gases out in all directions, which, as they cooled, formed the stars and the planets. All the galaxies are still moving away from each other as they cool. Since the invention of powerful telescopes, evidence has been found to support the theory of the Big Bang. According to scientific calculations, the universe is about 18 billion years old.

The theory of evolution

Most scientists believe that the different animals and plants came into existence in the world through the processes of **evolution**. Evolution is a theory that was first made famous by **Charles Darwin**, following the discoveries he made on a voyage around the world in a ship called the Beagle. Darwin suggested that different species had developed gradually over many years, but had not all been created just as they look today when the world began.

The theory of evolution says that weaker plants and animals die out, and only the strong survive. This is known as **natural selection**. Darwin suggested that humans developed gradually and shared ancestors with apes. Other animals had once existed, and have now become extinct.

The theories of science are different from the stories of creation found in Genesis because the scientists say that the world and the people in it developed very slowly, over millions of years.

Test yourself

1 What is the name for the study of how the universe began?

2 How old do scientists believe the world is?

3 What was the Big Bang?

4 How do most scientists believe that people began?

Different Christian responses to the challenges of science

Check the facts

Sometimes it seems that science poses a big challenge to Christianity and to the Bible. **The most important challenge is probably to the Biblical teaching about creation. The story is found in Genesis 1:1–2:2** and it explains how each part of creation was made by God over a period of six days (see topic 60).

The scientific view

Scientists say that the Earth came into existence from a Big Bang in the universe many millions of years ago and that the life forms that inhabit the Earth now have evolved over a very long period of time, with the more successful ones living and the others going out of existence.

Reconciling views

Many Christians do not find a problem with these two views. They believe that the story in Genesis is a myth. It is an attempt by the writers of the Bible to explain the existence of the world in which they lived, and is not meant to be a detailed and accurate account. **The important point is that the world was created by God, however that happened.**

Some Christians have tried to find agreement between the story in Genesis and the scientific evidence by saying that a single day in the Bible account could be many thousands of years long.

The fundamentalist view

Christians who take a very literal, or fundamentalist, view of the Bible believe that every word in it is absolutely true. They believe that science is wrong because it is only the ideas of humans, while the Bible must be true because it is the word of God.

Miracles are another area where science and religion seem not to be able to agree.

Test yourself

1 Explain some of the major problems that can arise between religion and science.

2 How have different Christians attempted to explain the difference between biblical and scientific accounts of creation?

Broadcasts of Christian worship – the 'God slot'

Check the facts

The God Slot

When the BBC started regular television broadcasting in **1946**, it had religious programmes on Sundays between 10.30am and 12 noon and from 6.00pm until 7.00pm. These broadcasts became known as the **God slot** and were almost always of entirely Christian content.

The BBC felt that it had a duty to provide religious programmes on Sunday and, because the United Kingdom was a Christian country, the programmes were designed to help people practise their faith. Most of the programmes were religious services, prayers, hymns and people talking about being a Christian and leading a Christian life.

As well as being suitable material to broadcast on a Sunday, people also saw the God slot as an opportunity to bring Christian worship into the homes of people who could not or did not go to church regularly.

In recent years, people have come to believe that religious programmes should reflect far more of the diversity of religious belief in this country and so there are programmes about the other major world religions. Also there are many more programmes on Sundays that are about religious and social ideas rather than just about worship. However, the majority of programmes broadcast in the God slot are still Christian.

Test yourself

1 What is the God slot and what was its original purpose?

2 Think about the sort of religious programmes that are broadcast today. What sort of religious broadcasting do you think should be put into the God slot?

Christianity and advertising

Check the facts

Advertising is something that you see and hear every day. **Most Christian churches use advertising to tell people about services, to encourage people to give money, to let people know about church clubs and societies they might like to join, and so on.** Some churches have advertising boards outside with a verse from the Bible on them to remind passers-by of the Christian message. In the Gospels, Jesus told his disciples to advertise the good news of Christianity.

Much of the advertising we see and hear from the media is trying to encourage us to buy products, or services such as mortgages and banking. **Some Christians, and other people, believe that advertising can be harmful because it encourages people to want things that they cannot afford.** It makes people think that everyone else is more successful than they are.

Advertising can give the impression that there is nothing wrong with being greedy. It makes people think that they have a right to have luxuries, even though many people in the world are starving.

Advertising can encourage prejudices. Television adverts very rarely show a black person testing a smart new car or using a washing powder. They very rarely show women tackling DIY jobs, or men changing nappies.

Advertising can make people feel uncomfortable about the way that they look, and especially about the shape of their body.

The **Advertising Standards Authority** tries to control the quality of the adverts that companies produce.

Test yourself

1 Give three reasons why some Christians might think that advertising can be harmful.

2 Explain three ways in which Christians use advertising.

3 What is the name of the authority which tries to control advertising?

Check the facts

Religion is a very important part of everyday life. Even people who do not have any religious belief find that many aspects of their daily lives, such as Sundays, holidays at Christmas and Easter, and the legal system are all strongly influenced by religion and, in particular, by Christianity. Because of this strong influence, it is not surprising that **many of the issues that appear in television soap operas and dramas are to do with religion in some way.**

Religion and ethical issues in soaps

There are many popular television soap operas and series, such as Brookside, Coronation Street, EastEnders, Family Affairs, Grange Hill, Hollyoaks and Neighbours. In all of these programmes, religion is sometimes discussed and becomes an important topic or storyline. Also, **many of the other storylines are concerned with ethical issues that have a religious dimension, such as abortion, euthanasia, pregnancy, marriage and divorce, theft, honesty and death.**

These programmes are designed to be entertaining rather than instructive and so they may not always present these issues in the way in which Christians would like. Quite often, religious people object to the storylines used because they believe that the media has a responsibility to uphold moral principles. The programme makers often respond to these complaints by saying that they are showing issues about real life.

Test yourself

1 What religious and ethical issues have been covered recently in soaps or dramas that you have seen?

2 Do you think that the producers of these programmes have a responsibility to educate people about the 'right' moral decisions that they should make?

The architecture of the church building

Check the facts

There are many different styles of church building. Some are highly decorated and dominate the landscape. Others are plain, undecorated and simple. The style of the church building usually reflects the way in which each denomination chooses to worship.

- **Roman Catholic and Anglican churches are often built in the shape of a cross, as a symbol of Christian belief.** The central part of the cross shape is known as the **nave**.
- Many churches have **spires or towers**, as a symbol of reaching up to God, and to make the building a prominent feature of the community.
- The most important part of Anglican and Roman Catholic churches is the **altar**, which is the holy table where the Eucharist is celebrated.
- In some churches, where preaching is believed to be very important, such as the **Methodist** church, the **pulpit** is the most important feature. It is a raised platform where the preacher stands so that everyone can hear him or her.
- Most churches have a place where people can be baptized. This is often a large bowl on a stand, called a **font**, but in some churches, where adults are baptized by going completely into the water, there may be a pool with steps going down into it.

Test yourself

1 What is the most important part of Roman Catholic and Anglican churches?

2 What is a font? What do some churches have instead of a font?

3 Why are many churches built in the shape of a cross?

4 Why do many churches have spires or towers?

Check the facts

The interior features of a church will vary according to the particular denomination to which the church belongs.

- The simplest type of Christian building is a **Quaker Meeting House**. The Quakers (Religious Society of Friends) do not have priests or ministers and do not have any special forms of worship. In their meetings they sit in silence until someone feels that God has something for them to say. Because of this style of worship, the meeting room is very plain, with just chairs and a table.
- Many **non-conformist or Protestant churches** have a large pulpit at the very front of the church from where the service is led, Bible readings take place and the sermon is preached. In front of this pulpit is a wooden table that is used for the service of Holy Communion. Somewhere in the church there will also be a font for baptism.
- **Anglican churches** are often more elaborate in their features. At the east end of the church, or sometimes in the very centre of the building, is the altar where the Eucharist is celebrated. The pulpit for sermons and the lectern for the Bible may be to either side of this. The font is usually placed at the west end of the church by the door.
- The most elaborate churches are usually Roman Catholic or Orthodox. In a **Roman Catholic church**, there may often be several altars, confessional boxes, statues and many candles. In an **Orthodox church**, the main feature is the iconostasis, or screen, that separates the main part of the church from the altar.

Test yourself

1 Choose two types of church and explain their main features.

2 Why are Meeting Houses so simple in their design and features?

3 Do you think churches should be elaborately decorated? Give reasons for your opinion.

The role of the church in the lives of Christians

Check the facts

The primary purpose of the church is for communal worship at services, on Sundays and sometimes also at other times during the week, such as morning services of Holy Communion.

Most Christians belong to a church in their local neighbourhood. The church provides a place away from the distractions of home, where Christians can get together with other believers and feel a sense of belonging to one group, and give each other support.

Christians also use the church in a variety of other ways:

- it is used for special occasions, such as **baptism, dedication, confirmation, marriage and funeral services**
- most churches have a variety of different social groups available, such as Parent and Toddler groups, Over-60s clubs and so on. The church can be the **social centre of a community**, particularly in rural areas
- statements from the churches about **moral issues** such as abortion can provide Christians with useful guidance
- the church can be used during the week for **private prayer**
- the vicar, priest or minister has a role in the community in **giving advice and support**
- the church can be a **focus for giving to charity** – its members might organise street collections, sponsored walks, fasts and so on.

Working together

Christians believe that the church is the body of Christ. This means that, together, they can be active in the world in the same way that Jesus was active when he was on Earth. The different members of the church have different roles, such as cleaning the building or providing the music, but all the different parts need to work together.

Test yourself

1 Name six ways in which a Christian might use his or her local church.

2 Explain why Christians have churches for worship, rather than just praying on their own at home.

3 What do Christians mean when they say that the church is the body of Christ?

Main differences in belief between Roman Catholics and Protestants

Check the facts

The Roman Catholic and Protestant denominations are the two largest groups of Christians. The Protestant denomination includes many churches, such as the Anglican church (Church of England), Baptists, Methodists and United Reformed Church.

In **1517**, Martin Luther was responsible for the beginning of the **Reformation.** He believed that much of the Roman Catholic church was corrupt and was not following God's teachings. The Reformation, which saw the division between the Roman Catholic and Protestant churches, was **a split away from Rome** (see topic 72).

The Roman Catholic church is based in Rome and has the Pope as its head. It is believed that the Pope is in a direct line from St Peter who founded the church in Rome and he therefore has the authority of the apostles of Jesus. The Pope is the spiritual leader of the Roman Catholic Church and is responsible for all the rulings and teachings that it issues. **The Protestant churches do not recognise the authority of the Pope and instead have their own religious leaders.**

As well as their belief in the spiritual authority of the Pope, **the Roman Catholic church believes in the intercessory power of the saints** and so prayers are said to, for example, the Virgin Mary, asking her to intercede with Jesus.

The Roman Catholic church also teaches **transubstantiation**. This means that when the bread and wine are consecrated at the Eucharist, they actually become the body and blood of Jesus.

Test yourself

1. Why was there a split between the Roman Catholic and Protestant churches?
2. Explain the role of the Pope.
3. Explain two major differences between Roman Catholic and Protestant teaching.

The importance of Mary for Roman Catholics

Check the facts

According to the Bible, Mary was a young woman betrothed, or engaged, to Joseph when she was visited by the angel Gabriel, who told her that she was going to conceive a son who was to be Jesus, by the power of the Holy Spirit. She did not understand how this could happen, because she was still a virgin, but she agreed to do whatever God wanted.

Roman Catholic and Orthodox Christians give Mary great honour because of her position as the mother of God's Son. They emphasise that they do not worship Mary, but they give her great respect and believe that she forms a special link between people on Earth and God in heaven.

They call Mary '**the Blessed Virgin Mary**', '**Queen of Heaven**', and '**Mother of God**'. They believe that if they pray to Mary, she will act on their behalf and present their prayers to Jesus. Many Roman Catholic, Orthodox and Anglican churches have a Lady Chapel, dedicated to Mary, where people can say prayers to her.

Roman Catholics and Orthodox Christians believe that Mary was born without sin and this is called the **Immaculate Conception**. They also believe that her body went up to heaven after she died and this is called the **Assumption**. Protestant Christians do not accept these beliefs.

Roman Catholics include a prayer to Mary as part of their daily prayers and weekly services:

> Hail Mary, full of grace, the Lord is with thee.
> Blessed art thou amongst women, and blessed
> is the fruit of thy womb Jesus.
> Holy Mary, Mother of God, pray for us sinners,
> now and at the hour of our death. Amen.

Test yourself

1 What might a Roman Catholic or Orthodox Christian say if asked whether he or she worshipped Mary?

2 Explain what is meant by: a) the Immaculate Conception; b) the Assumption of the Blessed Virgin Mary.

3 Why do Roman Catholics sometimes say prayers to Mary?

Check the facts

The word Pope comes from the Greek 'Pappas', meaning Father. It refers to the Bishop of Rome, the Head of the Roman Catholic Church.

Roman Catholics believe that the Pope is in a direct line of succession from Peter, who was chosen by Jesus to be the founder and head of the Christian Church. The position of Pope belongs to whoever is appointed as **Bishop of Rome**. Rome is the centre of the Roman Catholic Church because it was here that Peter and Paul became martyrs. Roman Catholics believe Peter passed on his authority to the next Pope, and so on.

The Pope is elected a few weeks after the death of the previous Pope by a group of clergymen known as the **College of Cardinals**. They discuss and vote in secret until a decision has been made.

The role of the Pope is to lead the Roman Catholic Church and to act as the representative of Christ in the world. He makes authoritative judgements and statements, appoints bishops and decides when they are to move to different places. He makes decisions about the right things to believe, once he has discussed them with the bishops.

The Pope lives in Vatican City in Rome. Vatican City was given to the Roman Catholic Church by the Italian government and it is a country on its own, so that the headquarters of the church are not in any one country.

In recent times, the Pope has visited many different countries around the world in an effort to unite the churches and to encourage people to follow traditional Catholic teachings and beliefs.

The Protestant churches do not accept the authority of the Pope. This is one of the main differences between Roman Catholics and Protestants.

Test yourself

1 Where does the Pope live?

2 Why do Roman Catholics believe that the Pope has authority over the church?

3 Explain in your own words the role of the Pope.

4 How do Protestant and Roman Catholic views about the Pope differ?

5 When the Pope dies, how is the next Pope chosen?

The Reformation

Check the facts

During the Middle Ages, the Church and its leaders were very powerful and many seemed to be more interested in making money for themselves than in following a Christian way of life. Members of the church were selling '**indulgences**', which were tokens that were supposed to give the buyer a better chance of getting into heaven more quickly. People were very superstitious and believed that, if they paid, they would suffer less punishment for their sins.

Martin Luther and John Calvin

A German priest named **Martin Luther** wrote out 95 '**theses**' or arguments against the way that the Church was behaving and nailed them to the door of the **Castle Church in Wittenberg** in **1517**. This is often thought to be the beginning of the **Reformation**.

Luther preached about how the Church had moved away from the teaching of the Bible and was taking advantage of the poor instead of looking after them. The leaders should have been serving the church members, not enjoying power over them.

Martin Luther and **John Calvin** became the leading thinkers of the Reformation. They taught that people would be saved by faith alone and not through good deeds. **They taught that the highest authority in Christianity was the Bible, not the Church and its leaders.** They argued that the Catholic priests were wrong.

The Reformation was a time when many Christians changed the way that they thought about sin and salvation.

Many historians believe that divisions between Roman Catholic and Protestant traditions can be traced back to the Reformation of sixteenth century Europe. The Roman Catholics still believed that the leadership of the Church was very important, but the Protestants did not accept this.

Test yourself

1 Which event is often thought to mark the beginning of the Reformation?

2 Why did Martin Luther object to the way that Church leaders were behaving?

3 What did Luther and Calvin think should be the highest authority in Christianity?

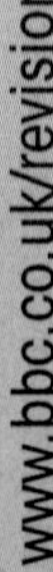

Check the facts

The word charismatic comes from the Greek 'charismata', which means 'spiritual gifts'.

The origins of the Charismatic movement are found in the Acts of the Apostles:

> When the day of Pentecost came, they were all together in one place. Suddenly a sound like the blowing of a violent wind came from heaven and filled the whole house where they were sitting. They saw what seemed to be tongues of fire that separated and came to rest on each of them. All of them were filled with the Holy Spirit and began to speak in other tongues as the Spirit enabled them.'
> (Acts 2:1–4)

People who belong to the movement believe that they are 'filled' with the Holy Spirit through the laying-on of hands. The signs of this include things such as:

- **speaking in tongues, or glossolalia**
- **prophecy**
- **and healing**.

As well as the Charismatic movement, which is found within many of the major churches, there is also a movement of **Pentecostal Churches** where people meet specifically because they wish to share and practise their gifts.

Test yourself

1 What is meant by 'charismatic worship'?

2 Explain the Biblical event associated with charismatic worship.

3 What is the difference between mainstream charismatic worship and Pentecostalism?

74 Evangelism and Christian mission

Check the facts

Christians believe that they have a duty to tell other people about their faith. This sharing of faith is called evangelism.

Some churches are known as evangelical churches because they put a lot of emphasis on sharing Christianity with other people. Evangelical Christians believe that the Bible holds 'good news' which they should share with others.

Jesus told his disciples:

> 'Go and make disciples of all nations, baptising them in the name of the Father, and of the Son and of the Holy Spirit, and teaching them to obey everything I have commanded you.'
> (Matthew 28:19)

Many Christians try to follow this teaching of Jesus by sharing their faith with the people they meet at school or at work.

Missionaries are people who go to non-Christian areas or countries to convert the people there to Christianity. They set up churches and encourage people to learn more about Jesus Christ and what it means to be a Christian.

In the past, missionaries sometimes went further than just telling people about Christianity. They tried to make people adopt Western clothing, culture and manners, and often did not think that there was anything of value in the religions that already existed in the countries they went to visit. Today, many people disagree with these aspects of the missionary movement. More people believe that different religions should respect each other's beliefs rather than assuming that other people are wrong.

Test yourself

Fill in the gaps with words that make sense:

1 People who go to non-Christian countries to convert the people to Christianity are called _____ .

2 Jesus told his followers that they should go out and make _____ of all nations.

3 Sharing the Christian faith with others is known as _____ .

4 Explain how attitudes to missionary work have changed in recent years.

Check the facts

The Orthodox church is one of the three major branches of Christianity, along with the Protestant and Roman Catholic churches, and is based on the Christian communities of the eastern Mediterranean.

The name **orthodox** means that the church follows the teachings of the apostles. It is probably the oldest part of the Christian church. **There are about 150 million members of the Orthodox church throughout the world.**

The Orthodox church is a group of independent churches, including the Russian and Greek Orthodox churches, who all acknowledge the 'primacy of honour' of the **Patriarch of Constantinople**, the head of the oldest part of the church. However, this is not the same authority as the Roman Catholic church gives to the Pope.

The central act of worship is the liturgy. This is a form of the Eucharist using very ancient texts that date from the earliest days of Christianity.

Icons

One of the most distinctive features of the Orthodox church is the use of **icons**. Religious art is very important to Orthodox Christians. **These icons convey the mystery of the Christian faith through art.** The icons are pictures of Christ and the saints and give people direct personal contact with the holy people represented on them. The images are venerated but not worshipped.

Test yourself

1 What is the Orthodox church?

2 Explain the importance of icons in the Orthodox church.

3 What is the liturgy?

The Society of Friends (Quakers)

Check the facts

The Society of Friends was founded by George Fox (1625–1691). Members are often called Quakers. This is a nickname given when George Fox told a judge that he ought to 'quake and fear' at the word of God, rather than be so proud.

The **Society of Friends** has a very simple, informal style of worship:

- They meet in plain buildings and the services are often conducted in silence, unless someone at the meeting feels that they have something to say. **They believe in sitting quietly and letting God speak to them.**
- **They believe that art and music do not help worship because it stops the worshippers from listening to God.** The meetings usually end with everyone shaking hands as a sign of their shared faith.
- **There are no priests or sacraments.** Early Quakers believed that ceremonies such as baptism and the Eucharist are a distraction rather than a help, although today they are more relaxed about this.
- There is no agreed list of beliefs that they must hold. People with all different kinds of beliefs can worship together. **Women have an equal role with men in the Society of Friends.**
- The Society of Friends is committed to non-violence. In wartime, most members will not fight but are **conscientious objectors**.
- They emphasise **sincerity and truthfulness.** They do not have moral rules about issues such as homosexuality, but believe that people should listen to their own consciences and do what they sincerely believe is right for them.

Test yourself

1 In which century did the Society of Friends begin?

2 Why is the Society of Friends often known as the Quakers?

3 Describe what a worship meeting of the Society of Friends might be like.

Check the facts

Christian worship varies widely across the world and also between the various denominations of the church.

- The simplest form of worship is found in the **Quakers (Religious Society of Friends)** where members sit in silence until one of them feels moved to speak.
- In most **Protestant** churches, the central act of worship is called the **Ministry of the Word**. This is the reading of texts from the Bible and a sermon based on these. Hymns and prayers also play a very important part in Protestant worship. Protestant churches celebrate the **Eucharist** less frequently than Roman Catholics – it is sometimes called the '**Lord's Supper**' or the **Communion**.
- In the **Roman Catholic and Orthodox** churches, the central form of worship is the Eucharist. There are, of course, services of Bible readings and prayers but the Eucharist is celebrated daily. This is often a very elaborate service.

The Eucharist is a very formal service where the priest, acting on behalf of the congregation, takes offerings of bread and wine and blesses them according to the instructions Jesus gave at the Last Supper:

> The Lord Jesus, on the night he was betrayed, took bread, and when he had given thanks, he broke it and said, 'This is my body, which is for you; do this in remembrance of me.' In the same way, after supper he took the cup, saying, 'This cup is the new covenant in my blood; do this, whenever you drink it, in remembrance of me.'
> (1 Corinthians 11:23–25)

The bread and wine is then distributed to the congregation.

Test yourself

1 What is the Ministry of the Word?

2 Explain the importance of the Eucharist.

3 Why do you think there are differences between the way in which Christians worship?

The Second Vatican Council

Check the facts

The Second Vatican Council was the twenty-first council called by the Roman Catholic Church. It was called by Pope John XXIII and sat from January 1959 until, after 178 meetings, it was closed by Pope Paul VI in December 1965.

The purpose of the Council was to work towards bringing the Roman Catholic church more in contact with the modern world. 2540 bishops and others attended the Council's meetings.

The topics discussed included:

- communications media
- the relations between Christians and Jews
- religious freedom
- the role of laity in the Church
- liturgical worship
- contacts with other Christians and with non-Christians
- the role and education of priests and bishops.

The theme of the Council was that the Church shared the '**joy and hope, the grief and anguish of contemporary humanity, particularly of the poor and afflicted**'. Local languages replaced the traditional Latin of the Mass.

The Council also said that it deplored '**all hatreds, persecutions, and displays of anti-Semitism levelled at any time or from any source against the Jews**'.

Most parts of the church welcomed the changes as bringing new life into their faith. However, there was some opposition, particularly to the changes in the Mass, and some Catholics formed themselves into separate groups who did not accept the rulings of the Council.

Test yourself

1 What was the purpose of the Second Vatican Council?

2 What topics were discussed at the meetings of the Council?

3 Explain the main outcomes of the Council and the way in which they were received.

Ecumenism and ecumenical communities

Check the facts

Ecumenism is the name given to the belief that all churches should try to become more united. It encourages Christians to worship together and forget their differences.

There are many issues which divide Christians and cause disagreements. These include:

- **The authority of the Pope** – some Christians believe that the Pope is the head of the Church and that Christians should accept his authority. Others disagree.
- **The ordination of women** – some Christians believe that women should have an equal role with men in Christian ministry. Others believe that men and women have different talents and that women should not be allowed to celebrate the Eucharist (Holy Communion).
- **The Eucharist** – some Christians believe that when the bread and wine are blessed by the priest, they really become the body and blood of Jesus. Other Christians think that they are symbols.

The World Council of Churches was set up in **1948** to promote ecumenism. Many Christians believe that it is important for Christians to work together because disagreements and divisions give a bad impression of the Christian message of love, and prevent Christians from doing important things, such as caring for the poor.

Ecumenical centres

Some ecumenical centres have been established, where Christians of all different denominations can worship together, no matter what church they come from. The **Taiz community** in France provides ecumenical worship for thousands of visitors every year. In the UK, the **abbey on the island of Iona** is used for youth camps and ecumenical worship. Both communities devote much of their time and income to helping the poor in developing countries.

Test yourself

1 What does ecumenism mean?

2 Name two places that are used as centres for ecumenical worship.

3 Explain some of the issues that cause divisions between Christians.

4 Why do many Christians believe that it is important to be united rather than divided?

The creed and the liturgy

Check the facts

The word 'creed' comes from the Latin 'credo', which means 'I believe'.

The Christian church has three creeds or statements of belief. The Apostles' Creed, the Nicene Creed and the Athanasian Creed.

The first two of these are recited regularly in church services as a statement of faith. The most often used is the **Apostles' Creed**:

I believe in God, the Father almighty,
creator of heaven and Earth.
I believe in Jesus Christ, his only Son, our Lord,
who was conceived by the Holy Spirit,
born of the Virgin Mary,
suffered under Pontius Pilate,
was crucified, died, and was buried;
he descended to the dead.
On the third day he rose again;
he ascended into heaven,
he is seated at the right hand of the Father,
and he will come to judge the living and the dead.
I believe in the Holy Spirit,
the holy catholic Church,
the communion of saints,
the forgiveness of sins,
the resurrection of the body,
and the life everlasting.
Amen.

The liturgy of the church is a set form of prayers and readings. This can be applied to any formal church service but is most often used about Eucharistic services.

Test yourself

1 What are the three creeds of the Church?

2 Explain what the Apostles' creed teaches about Jesus.

3 Why do you think it might be important to have a set liturgy?

The World Council of Churches

Check the facts

The World Council of Churches was formed after the Second World War, in 1948, by Christians who wanted to do something about restoring peace in the world.

It was set up to promote Christian unity, to act as a Christian voice in the world, and to help bring about peace and justice in accordance with Christian principles.

All of the main Christian Churches, apart from the Roman Catholic Church, belong to the World Council of Churches (WCC). They aim to listen to each other and to learn from each other in the hope that they will grow together rather than apart. They try to emphasise their shared beliefs as Christians rather than their different ways of worship and different understandings of aspects of Christian teaching.

The WCC holds meetings where members of all different denominations send representatives. They discuss all kinds of issues, such as:

- refugees
- the arms race
- ecumenism
- medical ethics
- world debt.

Christian Aid is the overseas aid agency for the World Council of Churches.

Test yourself

1 Which Christian denominations are members of the World Council of Churches?

2 What are its main aims?

3 Explain the sorts of issues that a meeting of the World Council of Churches might discuss.

Check the facts

Christians have many different names for the Eucharist. These include: the Lord's Supper, Mass, Holy Communion and the Breaking of Bread.

The word 'Eucharist' comes from the Greek meaning 'thanksgiving'. It remembers Jesus' last meal with his disciples before he was crucified:

> The Lord Jesus, on the night he was betrayed, took bread, and when he had given thanks, he broke it and said, 'This is my body, which is for you; do this in remembrance of me.' In the same way, after supper he took the cup, saying, 'This cup is the new covenant in my blood; do this, whenever you drink it, in remembrance of me.'
> (1 Corinthians 11:23–25)

For many Christians, sharing in the Eucharist is the most important part of their worship together because it means that they are united with each other as they share the body and blood of Christ. In some churches, the Eucharist is shared every day, but in others, it happens once a week, once a month, or even more rarely.

The celebration of the Eucharist usually follows a pattern:

- the bread and wine are placed on the altar and the priest or vicar reminds the congregation of what happened at the Last Supper
- the Eucharistic Prayer is said, giving thanks to God
- the bread and wine are blessed by the priest and the words of Jesus at the Last Supper are read
- in some churches, the congregation exchange a sign of peace
- the bread and wine are shared with the congregation
- the congregation are blessed and 'sent out into the world'.

Some Christians believe that the bread and wine become the body and blood of Jesus when they are blessed. Others believe that they symbolise Jesus' body and blood, but are bread and wine all the time.

Test yourself

1 What did Jesus say at the Last Supper when he broke bread and drank wine with his followers?

2 Give three alternative names for the Eucharist.

3 Why is the Eucharist such an important part of Christian worship?

Check the facts

Christians believe that, because of the disobedience of Adam and Eve in the Garden of Eden, all people are born with original sin. This sin needs to be removed before people can truly live their lives as Christians.

In some churches this cleansing of sin takes place when a young baby is baptised.

Our Lord Jesus Christ has told us
that to enter the kingdom of heaven
we must be born again of water and the Spirit,
and has given us baptism as the sign and seal of this new birth.
Here we are washed by the Holy Spirit and made clean.
Here we are clothed with Christ,
dying to sin that we may live his risen life.
As children of God, we have a new dignity
and God calls us to fullness of life.
(Common Worship)

As the baby is not able to speak for itself, **godparents** promise that they will bring up the child as a Christian. The priest or minister then blesses the baby and pours water over his or her head in the form of a cross, blessing the baby in the name of 'The Father, the Son and the Holy Spirit'.

Some Christians believe that baptism should only take place when people are able to make the decision for themselves. In the **Baptist** church, there is a ceremony of **adult baptism**. In the front of the church is a large tank or pool, covered by flooring. The pool is opened and the minister and the person to be baptised stand in it. The person is then baptised by total immersion. He or she leans back and is immersed under the water, held by the minister. **This is the sort of baptism that Jesus received from John the Baptist.**

Test yourself

1 What is meant by 'original sin'?

2 Why are people baptised?

3 Explain why some people choose adult baptism rather than the baptism of a baby?

Confirmation

Check the facts

Confirmation is a celebration of when people decide for themselves to follow the Christian faith.

If they were baptised as Christians when they were babies, then confirmation gives people the opportunity to confirm for themselves that the Christian religion is the one they choose to follow. They can make for themselves the promises that their parents and godparents made for them at baptism.

Not all Christian denominations have confirmation ceremonies because not all denominations have infant baptism. The churches that baptise adults do not feel that there is a need for an extra ceremony for them to confirm the promises they made at baptism.

Most people who are being confirmed prepare for this by going to confirmation classes. In these classes, they meet other people who are about to be confirmed and they learn about what it means to be a Christian and are taught about the promises they will make, so that they understand what they are promising.

A confirmation service is usually conducted by the Bishop.

- The Bishop asks the confirmation candidates questions: **Do you turn to Christ? Do you repent of all your sins? Do you believe and trust in God?**
- The candidates answer together.
- The Bishop places his hands on the head of each person being confirmed as a blessing. In some churches, he also puts some oil on their foreheads as a sign of the Holy Spirit.

Test yourself

1 Why do people go to confirmation classes before being confirmed?

2 Why do some Christian denominations not have confirmation at all?

3 Explain what happens at a confirmation service.

Check the facts

The Sacrament of Reconciliation, which is one of the seven sacraments, is a very important part of the life of the Roman Catholic church.

The Church accepts that everyone sins because they are human. Everyone needs to be freed from their sins to lead a Christian life.

Jesus taught his disciples that once they had received the Holy Spirit they had the power to forgive sins:

> And with that he breathed on them and said, 'Receive the Holy Spirit. If you forgive anyone his sins, they are forgiven; if you do not forgive them, they are not forgiven.' (John 20:22–23)

This power is believed to have been passed on to the priests of the church.

Confession and penance

Before receiving communion, Roman Catholics should go to church to make their confession. Usually they kneel in a small private space called a confessional. Here they can speak to the priest through a grille or a curtain.

When people confess their sins, they are usually given a penance to perform – this might be a practical duty they can carry out, or a set of prayers which they must recite. After the confession, the priest absolves them and says that their sins are forgiven. Whatever a priest hears in a confessional, he is not allowed to repeat to anyone else as he is only there as an agent of God.

Test yourself

1 What is the Sacrament of Reconciliation?

2 Why does a priest have the power to forgive sins?

3 Explain what is meant by penance.

Extreme unction

Check the facts

Extreme unction (or the last rites) is the fifth of the seven sacraments of the Roman Catholic Church. **It involves a blessing and anointing with holy oil for people who are ill, and especially for people who are in the last moments of life.** The priest asks God to forgive the person for any sins they have committed. The priest says:

> 'Through this holy unction and His own most tender mercy may the Lord pardon thee whatever sins or faults thou hast committed.'

The full sacrament is quite long and, in extreme cases, when death is likely before all the prayers have been said, a shortened version is allowed.

It is a sacrament that Roman Catholics believe has its origins in the Bible:

> 'They (the disciples) drove out many demons and anointed many sick people with oil and healed them.' (Mark 6:13)
>
> 'Is any one of you sick? He should call the elders of the church to pray over him and anoint him with oil in the name of the Lord. And the prayer offered in faith will make the sick person well; the Lord will raise him up. If he has sinned, he will be forgiven.' (James 5:14–15)

Roman Catholics believe that this sacrament is important because it encourages people to turn to God in the last moments of their lives. It helps to bring peace to people who are sick, and comforts relatives and friends of the dying, as the sacrament is a sign of God's forgiveness of sins.

Protestants do not accept that this sacrament is necessary.

Test yourself

1 How many sacraments are there in the Roman Catholic Church?

2 Why do Roman Catholics believe that the sacrament of extreme unction is important?

3 Where in the Bible are Christians encouraged to anoint people who are sick?

4 In what circumstances might the sacrament of extreme unction be shortened?

5 Explain what the priest says and does during this sacrament.

Check the facts

Ordination is one of the seven sacraments of the church. The others are baptism, confirmation, marriage, confession (reconciliation), the Eucharist and extreme unction (the last rites).

Ordination is usually when a person becomes a priest or minister of the church. After a period of preparation, someone who feels that he or she has a vocation to be a priest, presents him or herself to the bishop and asks to be ordained.

In the service of ordination, the bishop places his hands on the person to be ordained. This 'laying of hands' is to pass on the power of the Holy Spirit to the new priest and also to continue the **'Apostolic Succession'**.

The Apostolic Succession is a belief that the power of the Apostles was passed on by Peter and that there is an unbroken line of laying-on of hands from him to the present day. Therefore, the power of Jesus has directly been passed on for 2000 years, from one generation of priests to the next.

The Bishop says:

'Send down the Holy Spirit upon your servant 'N' for the office and work of a priest in your Church.'

Once the person has been ordained, they are themselves able to perform the sacraments.

Test yourself

1 Why do you think ordination is so important?

2 What is meant by the 'Apostolic Succession'?

3 Name three of the other sacraments.

Christian funeral services

Check the facts

Christians believe that death is not the end of a person, although it is the end of their life on Earth.

Christian funerals reflect this belief. Although people are sad because someone they loved has died, they are also encouraged to think about Jesus' promise of **resurrection**. They are encouraged to ask for God's comfort, and to thank God for the good qualities the person had, rather than concentrating only on sadness.

A Christian funeral is usually held a few days after a person has died, to allow time for people to be contacted and make arrangements to attend. Christianity does not have rules about whether people should be buried or cremated. This is a matter of preference.

The service begins with the vicar or priest reminding the congregation of the words of Jesus: 'I am the resurrection and the life'. There are always **prayers** thanking God for the life of the person who has died, and asking God to comfort the people who are left. There are often **hymns**, and **a talk** remembering the person who has died and the particular qualities that he or she had.

In Western societies, friends and relatives often wear dark clothes as a symbol of sadness, but this is a custom rather than a religious rule. Some people prefer to have an atmosphere of celebration for life, and wear ordinary clothes. It is also a custom to send flowers or wreaths to a funeral as a way of paying respect. When the coffin or the ashes are buried, the priest or vicar reminds people that we came from the ground when Adam was created, and return to the ground at death:

> 'We commit this body to the ground, earth to earth, ashes to ashes, dust to dust.'

Test yourself

1 How do Christian funerals demonstrate the belief that death is not the end of a person?

2 What are the main features of a Christian funeral service?

3 What might the prayers at a funeral be about?

4 How might a Christian funeral comfort the relatives and friends of the person who has died?

Check the facts

A pilgrimage is a religious journey, where people travel to places they believe have a special holy significance. They set aside time to make the journey because they want to get closer to God in a way that is not possible during ordinary working days.

Pilgrimage is more important to some Christians than others. **It is not compulsory for Christians** – some find it very helpful, and others never feel the need for it. In the Middle Ages, pilgrimage was very popular. **People travelled to cathedrals, such as St Albans and Canterbury**, to visit relics of the saints. **Some visited the Holy Land to see for themselves the places where Jesus lived, taught and died.**

Lourdes

Lourdes, in France, is a popular place of pilgrimage for Roman Catholics. It was here that the Virgin Mary is believed to have appeared to a young girl named Bernadette Soubirous. After Bernadette had seen these visions, a spring of water appeared and people began to report miraculous healings of illnesses and disabilities. Today, many people visit Lourdes, especially if they are ill, to go to where the Virgin Mary appeared and pray for healing.

Walsingham

Walsingham, in Norfolk, is another popular pilgrimage for Roman Catholics and Anglicans. In response to a vision, a replica of the house where Jesus was brought up by Mary and Joseph was built in Walsingham, and an underground spring was found. Although the Holy House was destroyed in the Reformation, people go there to pray and receive water from the well.

Test yourself

1 True or false?
- a) All Christians must go on a pilgrimage at least once a year.
- b) Some Christians never go on pilgrimages at all.
- c) A pilgrimage is a journey to a place of religious significance.
- d) Pilgrimage was more popular in the Middle Ages than it is today.
- e) A pilgrimage is no different from a holiday.

2 Explain in your own words the importance for Christians of either Lourdes or Walsingham.

3 What do Christians hope to gain from going on a pilgrimage?

The role of the priest/minister/vicar in the Christian community

Check the facts

The leader of a Christian community, whether they are called priest, minister or vicar, has an important responsibility to carry out

When a priest is ordained he or she is told that:

> 'A priest is called by God to work with the bishop and with his fellow-priests, as servant and shepherd among the people to whom he is sent. He is to proclaim the word of the Lord, to call his hearers to repentance, and in Christ's name to absolve, and to declare the forgiveness of sins. He is to baptize, and prepare the baptized for Confirmation. He is to preside at the celebration of the Holy Communion. He is to lead his people in prayer and worship, to intercede for them, to bless them in the name of the Lord, and to teach and encourage by word and example. He is to minister to the sick, and prepare the dying for their death.

These duties are based on Jesus' teaching, when he said:

> 'I am the good shepherd. The good shepherd lays down his life for the sheep. The hired hand is not the shepherd who owns the sheep. So when he sees the wolf coming, he abandons the sheep and runs away. Then the wolf attacks the flock and scatters it. The man runs away because he is a hired hand and cares nothing for the sheep. 'I am the good shepherd; I know my sheep and my sheep know me – just as the Father knows me and I know the Father – and I lay down my life for the sheep. I have other sheep that are not of this sheep pen. I must bring them also. They too will listen to my voice, and there shall be one flock and one shepherd (John 10:11–16).

Therefore the priest has to teach and lead the congregation as well as caring for them and trying to help them.

Test yourself

1 Explain the teaching of the Good Shepherd.

2 What are the main duties of a priest or minister?

3 How do you think a person can best carry out these duties?

Check the facts

Sunday is the main day of worship for Christians.

In the story of the creation in Genesis, it states:

> By the seventh day God had finished the work he had been doing; so on the seventh day he rested from all his work. And God blessed the seventh day and made it holy, because on it he rested from all the work of creating that he had done.
> (Genesis 2:2–3)

Then, in the Ten Commandments, God instructs the Israelites to:

> 'Remember the Sabbath day by keeping it holy. Six days you shall labour and do all your work, but the seventh day is a Sabbath to the Lord your God. On it you shall not do any work, neither you, nor your son or daughter, nor your manservant or maidservant, nor your animals, nor the alien within your gates. For in six days the Lord made the heavens and the Earth, the sea, and all that is in them, but he rested on the seventh day. Therefore the Lord blessed the Sabbath day and made it holy.
> (Exodus 20:8–11)

After the death and resurrection of Jesus, Christians decided that they would celebrate the Sabbath on a Sunday, the day on which Jesus rose from the dead, and the most important day in Christianity.

Test yourself

1 What are the origins of the Sabbath in the Old Testament?

2 Why does God order people not to work on the Sabbath?

3 Why do Christians celebrate the Sabbath on a Sunday?

The role of art and music in Christian worship

Check the facts

Art

Christians have different views about how art and music should be used in worship. **Some churches are very richly decorated. They have paintings, statues, stained glass windows, embroidered banners and kneelers, carved pews and lecterns,** and all the different kinds of art are presented as an offering to God and as a way of helping the worshippers to think about different aspects of God.

Eastern Orthodox churches, and some Roman Catholic and Anglican churches, use icons, which are small paintings or statues of Jesus and the saints, designed to focus the mind of the person who looks at them.

Other churches are much plainer. The Society of Friends, the Methodists, the Baptists and the United Reformed churches usually use much less art. Art is not forbidden, and there might be one or two examples, but the furnishing of the church is usually kept simple, so that the worshipper can concentrate on silence, or on what the preacher is saying, without being distracted.

Music

Most churches use some form of music in their worship. **The Society of Friends have meetings in silence,** but in other churches, music is used for hymns and for times of quietness and reflection, such as just before a service begins, or while everyone is receiving the Eucharist.

Traditional hymns help the congregation to remember that they are part of a tradition. They feel a sense of belonging when they sing hymns that their parents sang when they were children. Modern hymns help people to feel that the church is relevant to modern life and is a lively and vibrant part of the community. Some churches have choirs, to lead the singing of hymns and to make a more professional sound, as a way of giving God the best that people can offer.

Test yourself

1 Why are some churches highly decorated with all kinds of art?

2 Why are some churches plainer?

3 What are icons?

4 How might singing hymns together make Christians feel?

Check the facts

Prayer is a very important aspect of Christian life and worship.

- Some prayer is **petitionary**, asking God for something, for yourself or other people;
- **Intercessory prayer** may be to ask God to intervene in the world, at a time of crisis, for example.
- Many prayers, however, are **to thank God** for creation and for life and existence in general.

People may use formal, set prayers such as those found in the prayer books of the various churches. One of the most important of these is the **Lord's Prayer** which Jesus taught to his disciples (see page 26). Many Christians also use the **Jesus Prayer**:

Lord Jesus, Son of God
be merciful to me, a sinner.

Another very popular prayer, particularly amongst Roman Catholics is the Hail Mary:

Hail Mary, full of grace,
the Lord is with thee.
Blessed art thou among women
and blessed is the fruit of thy womb, Jesus.
Holy Mary, Mother of God,
pray for us sinners, now, and at the hour of our death.
Amen.

As well as using set prayers, many Christians may pray spontaneously, taking the opportunity to speak to God whenever they want to.

Test yourself

1 Explain the different types of prayer.

2 Name two popular prayers and explain their importance for Christians.

3 What is meant by spontaneous prayer?

Check the facts

Monks and nuns are people who have chosen to live apart from the world and to devote their lives wholly to God.

They live their lives very simply, away from society, at least in part, and **devote themselves to prayer, solitude and contemplation.** People take three vows when they enter a monastery or convent: **poverty, chastity and obedience.** This means that they have no possessions of their own, they are single and do not have any sexual relationships, and that they will always follow the rules and instructions given to them by the head of their order.

There are many different orders of monks and nuns:

- Some spend all their time in prayer and worship, believing that they can make a difference in the world by continual prayer to God.
- Some orders live in silence so that they can spend all their time thinking about God without distractions.
- Other communities live in the monastery but still work with the outside world, providing practical help for people.

All monks and nuns have to do practical work in the monastery, as they have to be self-sufficient. They grow their own vegetables, sometimes run farms, and make their own clothes.

The life of a monk or nun may be a retreat from the world, but it can be a very hard life, physically, and they are people who are prepared to sacrifice everything for God.

Test yourself

1 What are the three vows that monks and nuns have to take?

2 Explain the different sorts of lives that these people may lead.

3 Find out about one order of monks or nuns and see how they live their daily lives.

Check the facts

Christmas is one of the most important festivals of the Christian year. It celebrates the incarnation – the birth of Jesus, when God came to earth in human form.

In fact, no one knows exactly when Jesus was born, and it is more likely to have been in the spring than the winter. **The date of Christmas was not fixed until Pope Gregory did so in 354 CE.** Christmas was fixed at this time to absorb existing pagan festivals of the winter solstice on 21st December. It was also at the time of the Roman festival of Saturnalia and the northern European Yule festival.

Christmas traditions

Many of the things that we now associate with Christmas, such as holly, mistletoe and Yule logs, are taken from these pagan festivals:

- **The practice of putting models of the manger in churches was started by St Francis of Assisi.**
- Other traditions, such as Christmas trees, come from the nineteenth century.
- **The practice of giving presents has two origins.** Firstly, the festival of St Nicholas, the patron saint of children, takes place on 6th December and, secondly, the visit of the wise men to Bethlehem is celebrated by the Church on January 6th, the Epiphany.

However, most Christians send cards and give presents at Christmas. In addition, they often go to services at church, where they hear stories about the birth of Jesus, and sing carols.

Test yourself

1 What is meant by the 'incarnation'?

2 Explain why Christmas is celebrated on 25th December .

3 Explain the origins of some of the Christmas customs.

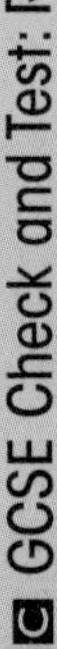

Festivals – Easter

Check the facts

Easter is the most important festival in the whole of the Christian year because it celebrates the resurrection of Jesus from the dead on Easter Sunday.

According to the gospel writers, on Easter Sunday morning, women went to the tomb where Jesus had been buried after his crucifixion on Good Friday. They had to go on Sunday, rather than Saturday, because Saturday was the Jewish Sabbath. The women went with spices in order to anoint Jesus' body.

When they got to the tomb, they found that the stone across the entrance had been rolled away and that the tomb was empty. They were told that Jesus had been raised from the dead. The details of the story are slightly different in each of the four gospels. **The resurrection is important for Christians because, for them, it proves that Jesus really was the Son of God, and has power over death.**

Easter is not always on the same date every year. It falls on the first Sunday after the first full moon after the Spring equinox. In some churches, Christians meet together on the evening of Easter Saturday and stay awake all night to pray. Traditionally, the first words that Christians say to each other on Easter Sunday morning are 'The Lord is risen', and the other person replies 'He is risen indeed'.

In some cultures, parents traditionally hide chocolate eggs for the children to find. **The eggs are a symbol of new life.** On Easter Sunday morning, the church bells are rung. The church is decorated with flowers and candles, which were put away during Lent, and the atmosphere of the service is one of celebration. **In some countries, there are processions and parades.**

Test yourself

1 Why is Easter the most important day of the Christian year?

2 Who first discovered that Jesus had risen from the dead?

3 What are the words that Christians traditionally say to each other on Easter Sunday morning?

4 Why do some Christians stay up all night on Easter Saturday until Easter Sunday morning?

5 At what time of year is Easter?

6 What do chocolate Easter eggs symbolise?

Check the facts

Advent is the four-week period leading up to Christmas. It begins on St Andrew's Day (30th November) or the nearest Sunday.

The word Advent means 'arrival' and Advent is a period of preparation for the celebration of the incarnation and birth of Jesus at Christmas. **Advent marks the beginning of the Church's year.**

Advent is a solemn season and in the past it was celebrated in the same way as Lent, with fasting and penitence.

There are several customs associated with Advent. One is making **Advent wreaths**. These are rings of evergreens, such as holly and ivy, with four red candles in them. One candle is lit on each Sunday of Advent until, at Christmas, all four are burning. In Britain, it was traditional to make **Christmas puddings** before the beginning of Advent and these were usually made on Stir-up Sunday, the last Sunday before Advent.

Services in Advent have special hymns and prayers as people look forward again to the celebration of Christmas.

Test yourself

1 Why is Advent still an important Christian festival?

2 Explain some of the Advent customs.

3 How has the celebration of Advent changed?

Festivals – Lent

Check the facts

Lent is the period leading up to Easter. It lasts for forty days, not including Sundays.

The forty days represent the forty days and nights that Jesus spent in the wilderness before he began his ministry. During this time, according to the Bible, Jesus was tempted by the Devil.

Lent is a time when Christians try to make themselves stronger against temptation, and prepare themselves for the celebration of Easter.

Shrove Tuesday is the last day before Lent begins. Traditionally, people eat pancakes to use up the last of luxury items, such as eggs and butter.

Lent begins with **Ash Wednesday**. Crosses made out of palm leaves for **Palm Sunday** are burnt and the ashes are used to make the sign of a cross on people's foreheads when they go to church. This shows that they are sorry for their sins.

In the past, Christians used to give up fish and meat entirely during Lent. Today, most Christians do not fast strictly, but many give up a luxury such as alcohol or sweets.

During Lent, the decorations in a church may be taken away or covered up to show that this is a solemn time of year. They are replaced at the end of Lent, which is Easter, when the mood changes to one of celebration.

Test yourself

1 What is the day before Lent called, and what happens on this day?

2 What is the name of the first day of Lent?

3 How long does Lent last, and what does this length of time represent?

4 What are Christians supposed to think about during Lent?

5 Why do many churches cover up their decorations during Lent?

6 What is the festival which immediately follows Lent?

Check the facts

Holy Week is the week leading up to Easter Day.

Palm Sunday

The week begins with **Palm Sunday**. This remembers the day when Jesus rode into Jerusalem on the back of a donkey. The people waved palm branches and laid them on the ground for the donkey to walk over. **Today, people who go to church on Palm Sunday are given small crosses made of palm leaves.**

Maundy Thursday

The Thursday of Holy Week is called **Maundy Thursday**. Christians remember the Last Supper that Jesus ate with his disciples. At the beginning of the meal he washed his disciples' feet and then shared food with them for the last time. Christians celebrate Maundy Thursday by remembering the Last Supper that is recalled in every celebration of the Eucharist.

Good Friday

The following day is **Good Friday**. Jesus had been arrested in the evening while he was praying in the **Garden of Gethsemane**. He was tried by several people and finally on the Friday morning he was sentenced to death. **He hung on the cross from noon until three o'clock, when he died. Many Christians spend these three hours in church praying on Good Friday.** Some people walk through the streets carrying a cross. After his death, Jesus was placed in a tomb and the doorway was sealed with a stone. This had to be done quickly because the Jewish Sabbath was about to begin.

Holy Saturday

Many Christians spend the next day, **Holy Saturday**, preparing the church by cleaning it and decorating it with flowers, ready for midnight when they begin the celebration of Easter and Jesus' resurrection from the dead.

Test yourself

1 What are the three most important days in Holy Week?

2 Explain why Maundy Thursday is so important for Christians.

3 Explain how people may observe Good Friday.

100 Festivals – Ascension Day and Pentecost

Check the facts

Ascension Day is celebrated on the Thursday that falls forty days after Easter Sunday.

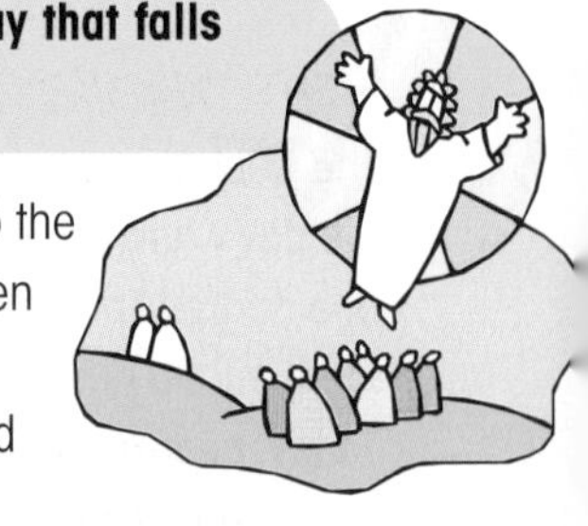

It commemorates Jesus' ascension, when, according to the Bible, he was taken up into heaven. After Jesus had been raised from the dead, he met his disciples and ate and talked with them, until he was taken up into heaven and they did not see him on Earth again.

Pentecost is a Jewish festival seven weeks after Passover. Christians celebrate it seven weeks after Easter.

It was at the celebration of this festival that Christians first received the Holy Spirit, according to the Acts of the Apostles. The Holy Spirit appeared as tongues of flame over them as they were assembled to celebrate Pentecost.

Pentecost is also known as 'Whitsun' or 'White Sunday' because of the white clothes that people used to wear as a sign of purity.

Pentecost or Whitsun is known as the birthday of the church because once Christians had the power of the Holy Spirit they were able to spread the message of Christianity. **Pentecost is traditionally a day for baptisms.** In some communities it is a tradition to take part in walks as a demonstration of faith.

Test yourself

1 What does Ascension Day celebrate?

2 On what day of the week is Ascension Day?

3 On what day of the week is Pentecost?

4 Why is Pentecost also known as Whitsun?

5 Why is Pentecost known as the birthday of the Church?

6 In which book of the Bible is the story of how the Holy Spirit was received at Pentecost found?

Central beliefs

01 The life of Jesus

1 Choose any two events from Jesus' life, including the Virgin Birth, baptism, temptations, ministry, death and resurrection. The important thing is to explain why you think they are still important for Christians today.

2 Think carefully about your answer to this question. One reason was that the Jewish priests were alarmed by the claim that Jesus was the Messiah. They expected the Messiah to be a kingwith an army to free them from Roman rule, and Jesus, who was nothing at all like this, was a threat to their authority and power.

02 What Christians believe about Jesus

1 They mean he is the 'anointed one' chosen and blessed by God.

2 They mean that Jesus is God in human form.

3 They believe that the death of Jesus was a sacrifice that made it possible for humanity to have a complete relationship with God, because their sins could be forgiven.

4 Belief in the resurrection is important for Christians because it proved Jesus really was the Son of God, and it gave them new hope of eternal life.

03 The doctrine of the Trinity

1 (a) The creator of the universe; a loving person we can depend on.
(b) Jesus; God in human form.
(c) God living in the hearts and minds of believers.

2 They might say they are monotheists, and the Trinity is a way to understand different aspects of the nature of God.

04 Agape

1 (a) Love the Lord your God with all your heart and with all your soul and with all your mind and with all your strength.
(b) Love your neighbour as yourself.

2 Do to others what you would have them do to you.

3 Agape is love that has no conditions, but is for everyone. It involves wanting the best for the other person, and treating other people as equals because they are part of God's creation. It is believed to be the way that God loves people.

05 The soul and the sanctity of life

1 Life is sacred because it is given by God.

2 It means that God creates life and God ends life.

3 They believe that their souls were made in the image of God so that when people die their bodies decay but their souls go back to God.

06 Christian beliefs about life after death

1 Purgatory is a place between heaven and hell where people are punished before being allowed into heaven.

2 Christians believe that, if they have accepted Jesus as the Messiah and lived according to his teachings, they will go to heaven when they die.

3 You need to explain that there are different ideas about heaven and hell e.g. some people believe in a hell with fire and devils; other people believe that it is a state where you are always deprived of being with God.

07 Beliefs about the nature of God

1 (a) Above and beyond the universe
(b) All-powerful
(c) All-knowing

2 The doctrine of the Trinity.

3 Monotheism

08 Christian beliefs about sin and salvation

1 Sin is to act against the will of God
2 You should mention the Ten Commandments and the two Great Commandments given by Jesus.
3 When Jesus willingly died on the cross he 'atoned' for people's sins. This means that everyone who believes that Jesus is the Son of God, and follows his teachings, is freed from the punishment of their sins. They are forgiven by God and so receive salvation.

09 Christian attitudes towards other world religions

1 Some Christians think Jesus taught that Christianity is the only true religion and there was no point in him dying on the cross if there were already other ways to get to God.
2 Missionaries go and try to persuade people to convert to Christianity.
3 Some people think that Christians can learn from members of other religions, and that talking together encourages people to live peacefully.

10 The relation between Christianity and Judaism

1 IThink carefully about your answer. It's important to remember that Jesus was Jewish, as this is how we can understand much of his life and teachings, as well as being the reason that he was crucified.
2 Jesus' followers believed he was the Messiah who is talked about in the Old Testament and who would come to release the Jews from persecution.
3 A Christian is someone who follows the teachings of Jesus Christ and believes that he is the Messiah.

Why do Christians believe in God?

11 Reasons people give for belief in God

1 (a) The argument that the universe must have been started by something, and this must have been God.
(b) The argument that nature seems to be intelligently designed, and this designer must be God.
(c) The argument that we know right from wrong, therefore there must be a God who makes rules about right and wrong.
2 Any opinion you give will gain marks, but only if you explain it clearly and give reasons. Award marks for words such as 'because' or 'therefore'.

12 Religious experiences

1 A religious experiences is when people feel that they have contact with something which is to do with God rather than with the physical world in which they live.
2 Discuss two types of religious experience e.g.visions, miracles, an experience of the numinous.
3 You are being asked for your own opinion; consider carefully why some people might believe that miracles still happen, whilst others might not.

13 Miracles

1 Something might be called a miracle if it is unexpected, goes against the laws of nature and is done by God for a special reason.
2 From the Old Testament e.g:
The parting of the Red Sea (Exodus 14)
Manna in the wilderness (Exodus 16)
The fall of Jericho (Joshua 6)
Daniel is saved from the lions (Daniel 6)

From the New Testament e.g:
Jesus calms a storm (Matthew 8:23)
The feeding of the five thousand (Luke 9)
The raising of Jairus' daughter (Luke 8)
Jesus turns water into wine (John 2)

3 The miracle stories are meant to show God's love, power and control over events.
4 Christians today might go to Lourdes or to a healing service.

Sacred writings

14 The Bible

1 Christians believe that the Bible is the Word of God, so obeying the Bible is a way of obeying God.
2 Some Christians believe that the Bible was given by God, word for word, to the people who wrote it down and it is literally true. Others say that God gave the writers ideas, and they wrote in their own words, using their own understanding of the world.
3 At home, in school, in church, in Bible study groups, at ceremonies such as weddings and funerals.

15 The Old and New Testaments

1 Tenakh or Torah, Ketuvim, Nevi'im
2 Good news
3 Letters in the New Testament that provide guidance and encouragement to Christians

16 The Ten Commandments

1 A covenant is a bargain or an agreement.
2 b
3 (a) Any of:
You shall have no other gods;
You shall not worship idols;
You shall not misuse the name of God;
Remember the Sabbath day and keep it holy.
(b) Any of:
Honour your father and mother;
You shall not murder;
You shall not commit adultery;
You shall not steal;
You shall not give false testimony against your neighbour;
You shall not covet (be envious of) your neighbour's possessions.
4 The Ten Commandments are important because they are believed to have come directly from God.

17 The Sermon on the Mount

1 In and around Galilee
2 Peacemakers
3 Because it was taught by Jesus
4 Forgive them

18 The Good Samaritan

1 A parable is a story that is told to teach a message.
2 There are lots of other examples e.g: The Parable of the Lost Son, the Parable of the Sheep and the Goats, the Parable of the Sower or the Parable of the Rich Fool.
3 The parable of the Good Samaritan could be used to show that Jesus taught that all people are neighbours, whatever their ethnic origin. It is the character of the person that matters.

19 The Sheep and the Goats

1 The Sheep are righteous people and the Goats are unrighteous people.
2 Feed the hungry, give drink to the thirsty, invite in strangers, clothe the naked, look after the sick and visit people in prison.
3 It teaches that that Christians should always look after those who are less fortunate than themselves, as this is what God wants.

Medical ethics

20 What is abortion?

1 (a) An abortion because of a deliberate choice to end a pregnancy
(b) An abortion carried out illegally
(c) Capable of surviving on its own
2 It is legal if two doctors agree that the health of the mother or her existing children would be harmed if the pregnancy continued, or if the foetus is seriously abnormal. The law allows abortions only up to the twenty-fourth week of pregnancy, unless the mother's life is at risk.
3 Give your own views here. Give examples of circumstances and also give your reasons. If you forgot to give reasons, count your answer as wrong.

21 Roman Catholic views about abortion

1 (a) The Roman Catholic Church says that abortion is wrong.
(b) They believe it is killing a person and only God has the right to do this.
2 'Before I formed you in the womb I knew you' (Jeremiah 1:5)
'For you created my inmost being; you knit me together in my mother's womb' (Psalm 139:13)
3 If it is essential for the mother to have an operation, not an abortion, and the effect of that operation is that the foetus will unavoidably die, then this is permitted.

22 Other denominations' views about abortion

1 The Anglican Church and the United Reformed Church
2 (a) This means that it is a personal decision and not a thing the Church makes an absolute rule about.
(b) The Roman Catholic Church teaches that abortion can never be justified.

23 What is euthanasia?

1 When someone chooses euthanasia for themselves
2 When euthanasia is forced on someone
3 When someone is given a drug or treatment that will end their life
4 When someone is allowed to die by, for example, withholding treatment from them

24 Roman Catholic views about euthanasia

1 They believe that every human life is made in the image of God, and that euthanasia is murder because it takes away God's gift of life.
2 Roman Catholics believe that suffering can sometimes help people to understand the suffering of Christ and to grow closer to God.
3 The law of 'double effect' means that an action can be acceptable if it happens as a side-effect of something that was meant to help, such as pain relief.

25 Other denominations' views about euthanasia

1 A document signed by someone saying that they don't wish to be kept alive if there's no hope of recovery
2 So that someone's suffering is ended
3 If, for example, patients would have to endure painful treatments and will still not recover from the illness

26 The hospice movement

1 Cicely Saunders founded St. Joseph's Hospice, in 1967.
2 Hospices aim to give care for the terminally ill and their families, and to help people to die with dignity, free from pain and worries.
3 Christians might prefer hospices because they avoid any need for taking away human life, which they believe is made in the image of God.

27 Roman Catholic and other views about contraception

1 Marriage should be 'unitive' (bring the couple close together) and 'procreative'.
2 The 'Rhythm Method' – the couple only have intercourse at those times of the month when the woman is unlikely to become pregnant.

28 Christian views about fertility treatment

1 (a) AID is Artificial Insemination by Donor. Sperm is donated by an anonymous man.
(b) AIH is Artificial Insemination by Husband. The egg and the sperm come from the couple.
(c) IVF is In Vitro Fertilisation. The egg and sperm are brought together for fertilisation in a laboratory rather than inside the woman's body. Donor eggs from another woman can be used.
2 They mean that life is a special gift from God and should be respected.
3 They might feel that this would introduce a third adult into the marriage, or that it might cause problems for the child in later life.
4 They might believe that these embryos are still human lives, and should not be destroyed or used in experiments, but protected.

Global ethics

29 The work of Christian aid agencies

1 'And if you spend yourselves on behalf of the hungry and satisfy the needs of the oppressed, then your light will rise in the darkness, and your night will become like the noonday' (Isaiah 58:10)
'Love the Lord your God with all your heart and with all your soul and with all your mind and with all your strength... Love your neighbour as yourself' (Mark 12:30-31)

2 Christian Aid; Caritas; Tearfund; Cafod.

3 They believe that people should not just be given aid and charity during disasters, but should be helped to become skilled and self-sufficient so that they can take care of themselves.

30 The use of wealth

1 He meant that it is impossible to be equally faithful to two different aims, and people who are keen on making money will find it difficult to devote themselves to God as well.

2 Some feel it's important to give the best to God and to worship in beautiful surroundings. Others think that God wants them to give everything they can to the poor.

3 (a) ...love his brother.
(b) ...you did for me.
(c) ...what you would have them do to you.
(d) ...is the root of all evil.

31 The work of Mother Theresa

1 You should give information about where she was born, when she became a nun, why she went to India and how she set up her order.

2 The Missionaries of Charity

3 Poverty, chastity, obedience and service to the poor

32 The environment

1 (a) Harming the environment with rubbish, chemical spillages, etc.
(b) Cutting down rainforests and clearing the land for other uses
(c) Resources, such as coal, that cannot be replaced, once used
(d) Changes in the climate as a result of a change in the balance of gases in the atmosphere.

2 Any of these (or your own ideas: Using 'green' products e.g. cleaner fuel; recycling paper, glass, etc; buying furniture made from renewable materials rather than scarce resources; cutting down on tuse of electricity, gas and coal; voting for parliamentary candidates who promise to pay attention to environmental issues; campaigning on local issues; using public transport, car sharing or cycling to work; reducing the rubbish they produce; joining an organisation which campaigns for the environment.

33 Stewardship – what it means in the Bible

1 Someone who looks after something for someone else.

2 The teaching in Genesis where God commands Adam and Eve to: "Be fruitful and increase in number; fill the Earth and subdue it. Rule over the fish of the sea and the birds of the air and over every living creature that moves on the ground."

3 The Roman Catholic church believes that all people should respect, care for and share the Earth's resources. Quakers believe that the produce of the Earth is a gift from God and that to impoverish the Earth is an injury to people in the future.

34 Christian teaching about animal rights

1 Christians believe that humans have souls, but animals don't, and therefore human life is sacred but not animal life.

2 (a) They might say that it is wrong to kill other creatures just for sport; or they might say that humans were meant to rule other animals, and that foxes are a pest

(b) They might say that it is wrong to kill animals for fur when there are other kinds of warm clothing available. They might say it is wrong to spend money on expensive clothes when there are starving people in the world. Or they might say that animals were put in the world for our benefit, and that we should be able to wear fur if we want to.

(c)They might say that Jesus ate fish and probably meat as well, and that there is nothing wrong with it. They might say it is a personal decision.

(d) They would probably say that it is more important to save a human life than an animal life, and that some testing is necessary but it should never be cruel.

3 Christians believe that all of the world is God's creation, and therefore they should respect and care for animals. People are the stewards of the Earth, which means they should have a care-taking role, not a destructive one.

Racism and equality

35 Racism and apartheid

1 Racism is putting into practice beliefs about discrimination. Some people think that others are different and inferior to them because of their race or the colour of their skin.

2 Some people are racist because they are afraid of people who are different from them.

3 Your answer needs to explain that apartheid was strict discrimination between black, coloured and white people in South Africa and that it left black people powerless and poor.

36 Biblical teaching about racism and equality

1 It means strangers, foreigners, or immigrants from another country.

2 (a) ...don't show favouritism.

(b) ...for you are all one in Christ Jesus.

(c) ...one of your native-born.

37 Martin Luther King Jr and Trevor Huddleston

1 You need to explain that they both felt that racism was evil and that God wanted them to work so that everyone could have a better life.

2 You might refer to Jesus saying that people should love our neighbours, or Paul saying that everyone who believed in Jesus was equal.

Ethics in relationships

38 Marriage

1. Christians believe that marriage exists so that two people can be together as partners, and so that children can be brought into the world in the context of a loving family.
2. They mean that a Christian marriage is a symbol of the love between God and humanity.
3. The bride and groom promise to love, honour and comfort each other, and be faithful to each other for the rest of their lives.
4. They expect to stay committed to each other for life (monogamy).

39 Roman Catholic and other views about marriage after divorce

1. Divorce is a last resort because marriage is sacred and is blessed by God so the marriage vows should never be broken.
2. An annulment means that the marriage was flawed in some way and therefore never really took place.
3. You need to explain a view such as that of the Roman Catholic church, which does not allow divorce, and one such as that of the Church of England, which sees that in some circumstances divorce may be the only option.

40 The family

1. (a) false
   (b) false
   (c) true
   (d) false
2. It says that they are worse than unbelievers.
3. Christians believe that children learn about love, forgiveness, and tolerance, and also learn about Christian beliefs, traditions and morality.

41 Care for the elderly

1. You should use teachings such as:
   'Honour your father and your mother, so that you may live long in the land the Lord your God is giving you.' (Exodus 20:12)
   'If anyone does not provide for his relatives, and especially for his immediate family, he has denied the faith and is worse than an unbeliever.' (1 Timothy 5:8)
2. Charities work in two ways: by providing practical help and also by acting as a pressure group on the government to improve pensions and care for the elderly and to fight ageism at work and elsewhere.

Personal ethics

42 Christian attitudes towards sex and sexuality

1 Because they believe that the sexual relationship between a man and a woman is a gift from God, which should give them both pleasure and can lead to the gift of children to the couple.

2 You need to have considered the different views of, for example, the Church of England and the Quakers about how homosexual people should be regarded.

43 Drugs, smoking and alcohol

1 Don't you know that you yourselves are God's temple and that God's Spirit lives in you? (1 Corinthians 3:16)

2 Any of the following:
They are expensive, and the money could go to the poor.
They can lead people into debt.
They cause health problems and show disrespect for God's gift of life.
They can cause family problems.
They can lead to domestic violence.
They are addictive.

3 The Salvation Army and the Methodists.

The disadvantaged

44 Care for the disabled

1 Christians have a duty to protect the weak; the Bible teaches that they should care for others; Jesus showed concern for people, and Christians should follow his example.

2 Mencap helps people with learning disabilities, and their families, by giving respite care, housing, education, and campaigning for rights.

3 Leonard Cheshire and Sue Ryder (you might also know of others).

4 You could use: 'In everything, do to others what you would have them do to you.' You might be able to think of other examples of your own.

45 Homelessness and the work of the Salvation Army

1 The Salvation Army follows Jesus' teachings in the Parable of the Sheep and the Goats.

2 The Army was founded to spread the Christian Faith and to help the poorest people of London.

3 The Salvation Army runs schools, maternity homes and children's homes, as well as still providing hostels with free lodging and free meals.

46 Suicide

1 In the past, people used to think that suicide was a form of murder, but now that they understand more about mental health issues, they are more sympathetic.

2 Christians think that life is sacred and a gift from God, and that people should not take it away.

3 Christians might support organisations such as the Samaritans as a way of showing concern for people in despair, and as a way of preventing suicide.

4 The Samaritans is run by volunteers; it offers confidential counselling on the telephone, by e-mail and face-to-face.

Gender issues

47 Are men and women equal?

1 In your answer you need to explain that the Bible teaches different things about equality between men and women.
2 You might suggest that in some churches they believe that men and women are equally suitable to be priests or ministers, whilst other churches disagree.
3 You need to explain the teaching that 'Each of the two sexes is an image of the power and tenderness of God, with equal dignity though in a different way'.

48 Women in the church

1 The Salvation Army and the United Reformed Church – you might also know of other examples.
2 The Roman Catholic Church and the Orthodox Churches
3 1994
4 Some people think that because the priest represents Christ, and because Jesus chose only men as his disciples, the priesthood is therefore not appropriate for women.

War, peace and justice

49 The just war

1 It must be fought by a legally recognised authority such as a government. The cause of the war must be just. The war must be fought with the intention to establish good or correct evil. There must be a reasonable chance of success. The war must be the last resort (after all diplomatic negotiations etc. have been tried and have failed). Only sufficient force must be used and civilians must not be involved.
2 In your answer, you need to have considered some recent or current wars and tried to decide whether they meet the conditions for a just war.

50 Biblical teaching about war and violence

1 Different parts of the Bible were written at different times and in different circumstances.
2 Jesus overturned the tables of the money-changers in the Temple.
3 You might have chosen:
'No-one will be able to stand up against you; you will destroy them.'
'Proclaim this among the nations; prepare for war!'
And:
'Blessed are the peacemakers.'
'Love your enemies, and pray for those who persecute you.'

51 Christians and pacifism

1 This is a question in which you need to decide for yourself, based on the biblical evidence, whether Jesus was really a pacifist.
2 Quakers are totally opposed to fighting and, during warfare, they are 'conscientious objectors'. They are prepared to go into battle driving ambulances or doing other duties but they will not fight.

52 Non-violent protest

1. (a) The British occupation of India.
   (b) The unfair treatment of black Americans.
2. Marches, speeches, sit-ins, boycotts
3. Martin Luther King
4. Some people believe that using violence reduces you to the level of the people you disagree with.
5. Others think that sometimes violence is the only way to get justice done.

53 Human rights and prisoners of conscience, Amnesty International

1. The aims of Amnesty International are: 'to free all prisoners of conscience; ensure fair and prompt trials for political prisoners; abolish the death penalty, torture and other cruel treatment of prisoners; end political killings and "disappearances"; and oppose human rights abuses by opposition groups.'
2. Amnesty International works by setting up campaigns of letter-writing, publicity and protests so that people may become aware of particular human rights abuses.
3. Many Christians support its work because, by doing so, they are expressing their belief in the value of human life and showing agape.

54 Liberation theology

1. Central and South America
2. They have believed it was their Christian duty to defend the weak against oppression.
3. Some people think that Christians should face suffering with patience, and that Christians should not become too involved in politics or use violence.
4. Other people have been encouraged to fight against injustice in other ways, for example, the fight against apartheid in South Africa.

55 Biblical teaching about crime and punishment

1. You need to explain Old Testament teachings about punishment and how God said this should be done. Also, you need to explain that there are many instances where God forgives people in the Old Testament.
2. It means that if someone causes you to lose an eye, the most you can take back is one eye. It limits the punishment.
3. Jesus said that people should be forgiven 77 times. This means that people should always forgive.

56 Punishment

1. A possibility is The Howard League for Penal Reform – you might know of others.
2. The parable of the Sheep and the Goats
3. Deterrence – putting other people off committing the same crime; retribution – paying someone back for their crime; protection – keeping the rest of society safe; reformation – making the criminal into a better person.
4. Elizabeth Fry is famous for her pioneering work in prison reform.

57 Different Christian views about capital punishment

1. Punishing a person for a crime by killing them
2. Quakers are totally opposed to capital punishment and say that people should respect life rather than destroy it.
3. You need to explain that, although the Roman Catholic Church has never condemned all capital punishment, many of its bishops believe that it is wrong.

Evil and suffering

58 Why do people suffer?

1 If there is a God who is able to do anything and who loves humanity, why is there evil and suffering in the world?

2 The book of Job teaches that suffering can be a test, and it should be accepted patiently even if we do not know why it happens.

3 Irenaeus taught that God put evil and suffering in the world so that we could use our free will, and grow to maturity. Augustine taught that the world was made perfect but was spoiled by the disobedience of Adam and Eve. Your own view: give yourself a mark if you explained the reasons why you hold these opinions.

59 Beliefs about the Devil

1 Lucifer was an angel who tried to be as important as God and because of this sin he was thrown out of heaven.

2 Jesus encountered the Devil during his forty days in the wilderness.

3 Today, many people do not believe in the Devil but rather that the power that tempts people to do the wrong things is within each person.

Science and religion

60 Biblical ideas about creation

1 The order of creation is: the heavens and the Earth and night and day; the oceans and the sky; the land and the plants; the sun, moon and stars; everything that lives in the sea and also the birds; the animals and men and women.

2 God created men and women in his own image.

3 God rested, and for this reason, the fourth Commandment is 'Remember the Sabbath day and keep it holy'.

61 Scientific theories about the origins of the universe and of humanity

1 Cosmology

2 Scientists think the universe is about 18 billion years old.

3 The Big Bang was a massive explosion which started the universe, according to many scientists.

4 Most scientists think that people developed gradually, and evolved through the process of natural selection.

62 Different Christian responses to the challenges of science

1 You need to explain that scientific accounts are often very different from the account found in Genesis, and that miracles appear to show that God can break the laws of the universe.

2 In this question, you need to have looked at some of the ways in which Christians have tried to explain how the Bible and science can both be correct but in different ways.

Religion and the media

63 Broadcasts of Christian worship - the 'God slot'

1 When the BBC started regular television broadcasting in 1946, it had religious programmes on Sundays between 10:30am and 12 noon and from 6.00pm until 7.00pm. These broadcasts became known as the 'God slot' and were almost always of entirely Christian content.

2 This answer asks for your opinion. You need to think carefully about what sort of religious broadcasting should happen today.

64 Christianity and advertising

1 You might have included: advertising can encourage people to want things they cannot afford. It can reinforce prejudices. It can make people think that it is all right to be greedy. It can make people uncomfortable about the way they look.

2 You might have included: Churches advertise on noticeboards; they tell people about services, and encourage them to give money to charity; they tell people about organisations they might want to join.

3 The Advertising Standards Authority

65 Christianity and soaps/dramas

1 For this question, you need to think about television programmes you have seen recently and make a list of the ethical issues they have covered.

2 Here we are looking for your own opinion. Make sure that you give reasons to support what you say.

The Church

66 The architecture of the church building

1 The altar

2 A font is a basin used for baptism. Some churches have a pool instead, where people can get right inside.

3 It is a symbol of Christian belief.

4 Spires or towers can be a symbol of reaching up to God, and they are a way of showing the importance of the church in the community.

67 Interior features/artefacts of a church

1 You can choose any two types of church building. You need to say what denomination they belong to and then explain the importance of their features.

2 Your answer should explain that the Quakers (Religious Society of Friends) do not have priests or ministers and do not have any special forms of worship. In their meetings, they sit in silence until someone feels that God has something for them to say. Because of this style of worship the meeting room will be very plain with just chairs and a table.

3 This question asks for your opinion. Think carefully about your answer and remember to give reasons to support what you say.

68 The role of the church in the lives of Christians

1 You might have included: baptisms; confirmation; weddings; funerals; social clubs; moral guidance; private prayer; Sunday worship; a focus for charitable giving.

2 Christians believe that they can support each other if they worship as a group. It gives them the sense of belonging to a tradition.

3 They mean that they all have different roles, but can work together to do the work of Jesus in the world.

69 Main differences in belief between Roman Catholics and Protestants

1. In 1517, Martin Luther was responsible for the beginning of the Reformation. He believed that much of the Roman Catholic church was corrupt and was not following God's teachings. The Reformation, which saw the division between the Roman Catholic and Protestant churches, was a split away from Rome.
2. The Pope is the head of the Roman Catholic church. It is believed that the Pope is in a direct line from St Peter who founded the church in Rome and he therefore has the authority of the apostles of Jesus. Therefore, the Pope is the spiritual leader of the Roman Catholic Church and is responsible for all the rulings and teachings which it issues.
3. You may choose teachings about the eucharist, about the role of the Pope or the role of the saints. You need to explain these differences.

70 The importance of Mary for Roman Catholics

1. They would say that they don't worship Mary, but they give her great respect and honour as the woman chosen to be the mother of God's son.
2. (a) It is the belief that Mary was born without sin.
   (b) It is the belief that Mary was taken up into heaven after she died.
3. They believe that Mary has a special relationship with God and can present prayers on behalf of believers.

71 The role of the Pope

1. Vatican City, Rome
2. They believe he is the representative of Christ in the world, following on in a line of succession from the apostle Peter.
3. You could include ideas such as: appointing bishops; making decisions about belief; making statements about moral issues; travelling to different countries to encourage people in the faith.
4. Protestants do not accept the authority of the Pope.
5. The College of Cardinals discusses and votes in secret.

72 The Reformation

1. A German priest named Martin Luther wrote out 95 'theses', or arguments, against the way that the Church was behaving, and nailed them to the door of the Castle Church in Wittenberg in 1517.
2. Luther thought the Church had moved away from the teaching of the Bible, and was taking advantage of the poor instead of looking after them. The leaders should have been serving the church members, not enjoying power over them.
3. The Bible

73 The Charismatic movment

1. The word charismatic comes from the Greek 'charismata' which means 'spiritual gifts'. Charismatic worship includes speaking in tongues, or glossolalia, prophecy, and healing.
2. You need to explain the events of the first Pentecost when the Holy Spirit came down to the disciples.
3. The differences are that charismatic worship can be found as part of the worship in many mainstream churches, such as the Church of England. The Pentecostal churches are where people meet together specifically because they wish to share and practise their charismatic gifts.

74 Evangelism and Christian mission

1 Missionaries
2 Disciples
3 Evangelism
4 In the past, people were often convinced that Christianity was right and that members of other religions were wrong. Today, many people think that different religions should respect each other's beliefs rather than assume that other people are wrong.

75 Orthodox Christianity

1 The Orthodox church is one of the three major branches of Christianity and is based on the Christian communities of the eastern Mediterranean. The name 'orthodox' is used to mean that the church follows the teachings of the apostles. It is probably the oldest part of the Christian church.
2 Icons are pictures of Christ and the saints, and give people direct personal contact with the holy people represented on them. The images are venerated but not worshipped. They are used to convey the mystery of the Christian faith through art.
3 The liturgy is the name given to the celebration of the eucharist in Orthodox churches.

76 The Society of Friends (Quakers)

1 In the seventeenth century
2 It was because George Fox told a judge that he should quake and fear before God.
3 It might take place in total silence, or any member of the meeting might get up and speak.

77 Styles of worship in different denominations

1 This is the reading of texts from the Bible and a sermon based on these.
2 The Eucharist is very important in most churches because it remembers and celebrates the Last Supper which Jesus ate with his disciples.
3 Here you are being asked for your opinion. You need to think carefully about some of the differences in the ways in which Christians worship, and then explain them.

78 The Second Vatican Council

1 The purpose of the Council was to work towards bringing the Roman Catholic Church more in contact with the modern world.
2 The topics discussed included communications media, the relations between Christians and Jews, religious freedom, the role of laity in the Church, liturgical worship, contacts with other Christians and with non-Christians, and the role and education of priests and bishops.
3 You need to describe the outcomes and explain that most parts of the church welcomed the changes as bringing new life into their faith, whilst some people objected to the changes.

79 Ecumenism and the ecumenical communities

1 Ecumenism is the name given to the belief that all churches should try to become more united.
2 You could choose Taiz and Iona, or you might know of some other places.
3 You could include the following, or you might have your own ideas: the Eucharist; the authority of the Pope; interpretation of the Bible; the ordination of women.
4 They believe that Christians show a bad example if there are too many disagreements, and that more work gets done for other people if everyone works together.

80 The creed and the liturgy

1 The Apostles' Creed, the Nicene Creed and the Athanasian Creed.

2 That he was the son of God; he was conceived by the Holy Spirit, his mother was the Virgin Mary, he suffered under Pontius Pilate, he was crucified, died, and was buried, he descended to hell. On the third day he rose again, he ascended into heaven, he is seated at the right hand of God and he will come again to judge the living and the dead.

3 This question asks for your opinion. Think carefully about your answer and remember to give reasons for what you say.

81 The World Council of Churches

1 All of the main churches apart from the Roman Catholic Church.

2 It aims to encourage Christians of different denominations to work together for peace and justice for the poor.

3 You could include some of the following, or you might have your own ideas: refugees, the arms race, world debt, famine relief, medical ethics, ecumenism.

Sacraments

82 Eucharist

1 He said 'This is my body, which is for you; do this in remembrance of me.' 'This cup is the new covenant in my blood; do this, whenever you drink it, in remembrance of me.'

2 Mass; Holy Communion; the Lord's Supper; the Breaking of Bread

3 It is important because it is a sign of the unity of Christians as they share in the body and blood of Christ.

83 Baptism – infant and adult

1 Christians believe that, because of the disobedience of Adam and Eve in the Garden of Eden, all people are born with original sin.

2 People are baptised to be welcomed into the church and to be cleansed from original sin.

3 You need to explain that some Christians believe that baptism should only take place when a person is able to make the decision for themselves.

84 Confirmation

1 They learn about Christianity, so that they understand what they are promising.

2 Some churches baptise adults (believers' baptism) and so they do not need to confirm the promises that were made when they were babies.

3 The candidates are asked questions about their faith; the bishop places his hands on their heads to bless them and, in some churches, oil is placed on their forehead as a sign of the Holy Spirit.

85 Sacrament of reconciliation (RC)

1. The Sacrament of Reconciliation is a very important part of the life of the Roman Catholic Church. The church accepts that everyone sins because they are human, and reconciliation frees them from their sins to lead a Christian life.
2. Because Jesus gave this power to his disciples and it has been passed on from them to the priests of the church.
3. A penance is given by the priest when he forgives a person's sins. This might be a practical duty they can carry out, or a set of prayers which they must recite.

86 Extreme unction

1. Seven
2. It encourages people to turn to God in the last moments of their lives, and brings peace and comfort.
3. Mark 6:13; James 5:14-15
4. The sacrament might be shortened if the person seems likely to die very soon.
5. The priest anoints the sick person with oil, and asks God to forgive them for their sins.

87 Ordination

1. Ordination is important because it is when a person is given the power of the Holy Spirit and becomes a priest or minister of the church.
2. The Apostolic Succession is a belief that the power of the Apostles was passed on by Peter and that there is an unbroken line of laying-on of hands from him to the present day. Therefore, the power of Jesus has directly been passed on for 2000 years from one generation of priests to the next.
3. Baptism, confirmation, marriage, confession (reconciliation), the eucharist and extreme unction (the last rites).

88 Christian funeral services

1. They emphasise the hope of resurrection.
2. The priest reminds people that Jesus rose from the dead and that Christians hope for resurrection; there are prayers, and often hymns and a talk; the body is buried or cremated.
3. The prayers might thank God for the life of the person who has died, and ask for comfort for the friends and relatives.
4. It might remind them of their beliefs in life after death and in the love of God, and make them feel that death is not the end.

Christian life

89 Pilgrimage

1 (a) false
(b) true
(c) true
(d) true
(e) false

2 Your answer should say something about why the place is believed to be holy, and the sort of people who might visit it, and what they might do when they get there.

3 Christians hope to get closer to God in a way that is not possible in ordinary life. Sometimes they also hope for healing.

90 The role of the priest/minister/vicar in the Christian community

1 You need to explain Jesus' teaching that he was like a shepherd looking after his flock.

2 The main duties are: to proclaim the word of the Lord, to forgive, to baptize, to prepare people for Confirmation, to celebrate Holy Communion, to lead people in prayer, to pray for them, to bless them, to teach and encourage them, to minister to the sick, and prepare the dying for their death.

3 This question asks for your own opinion. Think carefully about your answer and remember to give reasons for what you think.

91 The importance of Sunday for Christians

1 You need to mention that God rested on the seventh day and also that, in the Ten Commandments, the Israelites were instructed to rest on the Sabbath.

2 God orders people not to work on the Sabbath because it is holy day, when he rested, and they should keep the Sabbath for God.

3 After the death and resurrection of Jesus, Christians decided that they would celebrate the Sabbath on a Sunday, the day on which Jesus rose from the dead, and the most important day in Christianity.

92 The role of art and music in Christian worship

1 Some Christians believe that art and music help the worshipper to concentrate on aspects of God's nature, and are a way of giving God the best that people can offer.

2 Some Christians believe that plainer churches are less of a distraction, and that worship should be simple.

3 Icons are paintings or statues of Jesus, Mary or the saints, used in worship by some Christians.

4 They might feel united as believers, and part of a tradition.

93 Prayer

1 You need to explain what is meant by: petitionary prayer, asking God for something for yourself or other people; intercessory prayer, asking God to intervene in the world at a time of crisis, for example; and prayers which are to thank God.

2 You need to choose two of the prayers which you have studied, for example, the Lord's Prayer and the Hail Mary, or the Jesus Prayer, and explain why Christians find these important.

3 Many Christians pray spontaneously, taking the opportunity to speak to God whenever they want to.

94 The monastic life

1 Poverty, chastity, and obedience

2 Some spend all their time in prayer, some live in silence so they can spend all their time thinking about God, others live at the monastery but work with the outside world

3 This question asks you to do some research. Think carefully about your answer and remember to give reasons for what you say.

The Christian year

95 Festivals - Christmas

1 The birth of Jesus; when God came to earth in human form.
2 It was fixed at this time to absorb existing pagan solstice festivals.
3 Some Christmas customs come from pagan festivals, others have developed over the last 2000 years.

96 Festivals - Easter

1 It celebrates the resurrection of Jesus.
2 The women who went to the tomb to anoint Jesus' body were the first to realise that he had risen from the dead.
3 'The Lord is risen'; 'He is risen indeed.'
4 Some Christians stay up all night to pray.
5 Easter is in the Spring (in the Northern hemisphere).
6 They symbolise new life.

97 Festivals - Advent

1 Advent is still important because it means 'arrival' and is a period of preparation for the celebration of the incarnation and birth of Jesus at Christmas.
2 You might choose to explain the customs of Advent wreaths and Stir-up Sunday.
3 You should explain that Advent is no longer celebrated in the same way as Lent as it was in the past.

98 Festivals – Lent

1 Shrove Tuesday; people traditionally use up luxury foods they have left in their houses, for example, by making pancakes.
2 Ash Wednesday
3 Forty days, not including Sundays - they represent the time Jesus spent in the wilderness before beginning his ministry.
4 Christians are supposed to think about repentance, and about Jesus' sacrifice on the cross.
5 They cover their decorations because it is a solemn time of year.
6 Easter

99 Holy Week and the Last Supper

1 Palm Sunday, Maundy Thursday, Good Friday
2 On Maundy Thursday, Christians remember the Last Supper which Jesus ate with his disciples. At the beginning of the meal he washed his disciples feet and then shared food with them for the last time. Christians celebrate Maundy Thursday by remembering the Last Supper which is recalled in every celebration of the Eucharist.
3 Many Christians spend the three hours when Jesus was on the cross praying in church. Other people may walk through the streets carrying a cross.

100 Festivals – Ascension Day and Pentecost

1 It celebrates the time when Jesus was taken into heaven after his resurrection.
2 Thursday
3 Sunday
4 It is known as Whitsun because traditionally, people wore white clothes on this day.
5 It is known as the birthday of the church because it was the day when people received the power of the Holy Spirit.
6 The Acts of the Apostles